Cats
Do Eat
Spaghetti

Paul Wright

"I love cats because I enjoy my home; and little by little, they become its visible soul."
Jean Cocteau

Dedicated to all the cats big and small in the world I love you all.

CONTENTS

Also by Paul Wright

The first book of the Italian trilogy is
An Italian Home - Settling by Lake Como

The sequel to An Italian Home is
An Italian Village - a Perspective on Life Beside Lake Como

About the Author

Paul Wright is an award-winning artist who specialises in Trompe l'Oeil murals, oil paintings and watercolour landscapes of Lake Como.

In 1982, following a period spent designing theatre sets around the UK, Paul started his own art studio in Surrey.

In 1991, he moved to northern Italy with his partner, Nicola, where he continues to write and paint from his studio base in the beautiful medieval village of Argegno on the shores of Lake Como, and from where he travels to other European countries and to the USA.

Paul's work has been featured in many art exhibitions in the UK and on two live programmes for Italian television, plus dozens of periodicals and newspapers worldwide, notably *The Sunday Times, Architectural Digest, The Wall Street Journal* and *The Arts Review.*

1 Whiskers

I was six and three quarters when I fell in love for the first time.

It happened on a bright Saturday morning one spring in our local Co-op grocery store. As part of my weekend chores I would go there to fetch a white tin loaf, four eggs, three tomatoes and a pound of streaky bacon. On that propitious Saturday, when Bob Jackson, the man who worked the bacon slicer placed the foodstuffs in my basket, he also deposited an eight month-old kitten along with them. 'Her name is Whiskers,' he announced. 'She needs a good home and I've chosen you to give it to her.'

I have only a vague recollection of what Whiskers actually looked like, but as far as I remember she was a shorthaired tabby, and she was gorgeous. My memory of her exact markings remains clouded, because nobody ever took a photograph of her, but I shall always remember with great fondness the occasion she was presented to me, because it was the moment I became an incurable ailurophile and I would relive this delightful experience at least another twenty times. (I discovered many years later an ailurophile is the name for a lover of cats).

Back in the late 1950s, I had two middle-class parents who, along with me, inhabited an almost new semi-detached house with rendered, cream painted walls. It was in a seaside town called Formby on the northwest coast of England, thirteen miles north of Liverpool. Formby was, and still is a spread out, appealing country town in the urban jurisdiction of Sefton in the old Shire of Lancaster, now called Merseyside.

Our semi was pretty much the same as the other twenty-eight in a crescent shaped, tree-lined road a mile inland. Typically, it was a mirror image of its other half and furnished in an equally typical way. Downstairs, off a spacious hallway was the lounge, containing a three-piece suite. Through the lounge door there was a separate dining room and off that, a small kitchen. A carpeted staircase led from the hall to three adequate sized bedrooms and a bathroom with a white glazed bath, toilet and washbasin. Every semi had a long back garden that, in general, the residents tended faithfully. The front gardens were shorter, with low brick walls and waist-high wooden front gates. Most had driveways. A few had carports and some had one-car garages, but the rest had nothing at all. Ours had a carport with a corrugated asbestos roof, but we had no car to go under it My father preferred a Vespa scooter, but neither my mother nor I liked riding pillion. We wanted him to buy a VW Beetle and after a great deal of persuasion he did.

I was the same age, almost to the day as Mary Eccles, the girl who lived in the semi next door and she had two cats. Unlike her, I wasn't the sort of child who had begged for a friend to keep. She pestered her parents unremittingly to present her with lots of friends who were prepared to share genuine warmth and love with her. Although I had thought many times about demanding that my parents found friends for me, I never did. Mary had more pets, including insects, reptiles, fish, rodents, and caged birds than almost all the residents of the crescent put together. The only thing she didn't have, but still wanted badly was a horse, but even her indulgent parents had to call a halt at some point. Only Tommy Aindow had more animals in his care. He had a coop full of racing pigeons, and my mother detested him for having them, because twice a day, Tommy would open the flaps to his coop to allow his cherished flock to exercise their wings. This meant that because of his birds' predisposition to soil her washing, hanging on the clothes line in our back garden my mother wanted to see both them and Tommy removed from this earth.

As a keen gardener, my father was averse to all creatures from the natural world, but in particular he was averse to Mary's dogs, cats and rabbits. He was also averse to Mary herself for not keeping them locked up. A wire-netting fence separated our garden from the Eccles's, which Mary's cats and dogs found easy to jump over. As he looked through the glass of the sliding patio doors to admire his pristine back garden and his meticulous vegetable patch beyond, he would always keep a broom close to hand, just in case one of Mary's pets was on the loose. And if any of her six rabbits had a fancy for some of his vegetables, they would burrow underneath the fence and do their best to gorge themselves. But because my father never seemed to comprehend that animals didn't recognise the same territorial boundaries that humans have, his wife, was convinced that the duress the animals caused him contributed to the stroke he would suffer later in life.

My mother was fixated by hygiene and she would clean the house until every part of it shone. She would not tolerate having any animal in the house, because she believed they all harboured germs. So on that Saturday morning, when I returned from the Co-op store with more than just food in my basket, she all but threw a fit. 'Get that thing out of this house, immediately!' She screamed.

When I took Whiskers outside and into my father's garden did she become rational, or as rational as she could be, which was never one hundred per cent, and the delight I radiated on that Saturday morning didn't convince her one bit that we should keep this furry little wonder that was sitting in the basket alongside the bread, eggs and tomatoes, licking herself clean. Only when I boo-hooed my eyes out did she give in and let the kitten stay. After all, that's what Mary Eccles did to get her own way and it always seemed to work for her. But sadly Whiskers was not to stay for very long.

After all, that's what Mary Eccles did to get her own way and it always seemed to work for her. For once, it worked for me, but sadly Whiskers was not to stay for very long.

I had never expected to be a cat owner (that is, as far as anyone can actually *own* a cat), probably because I'd been brainwashed from an early age into believing that only spoilt children have animals. Nice, unspoilt boys like me do not. Next door was held up as a case in point, because my parents regarded Mary as being spoilt to death - and nobody likes a spoilt child. Where I was rake thin, Mary was a fat dumpling of a kid, and I was instructed to believe that was how I would end up looking if I were ever spoilt. Sometimes I wished I was a titch spoilt and then, perhaps I would only be a little bit fatter.

After a lot of wrangling, my mother and I finally came to an agreement. As long as I was prepared to look after "it" and she didn't have any involvement with "it", then "it" could stay. Needless to say, there were supplementary conditions within the agreement that were so improbable and so long-winded I would never be able to remember them. Unfortunately, less than a fortnight after its creation, the agreement became untenable. My mother declared that she had pulled all her hair out over the behaviour of our new resident because, she said, it had been so naughty when I was at school. I guess Whiskers was branded as naughty for a couple of reasons. The first was because on one occasion she peed on the dining-room carpet, but this was because the door leading from the kitchen to the garden had been shut and she couldn't get out. Another reason concerned the lace curtains that adorned the sliding door windows in the lounge. The texture of these was made for plucking and, as I was informed, she plucked them at least five times a day while I was at school. I have to say I hadn't witnessed any of the plucking mentioned, or any evidence of the aforesaid plucking. But I *was* around when Whiskers leapt on the dining table to help herself to my dinner. She did it because, like me, she was underfed. In my mother's judgement, being underfed was healthier than being overfed and she applied the same philosophy to Whiskers. The second time Whiskers tried to indicate to her that living with us constituted starvation was when she leapt on the dining table once more and stole a chump chop off my mother's plate, just as she was about to cut into it. That prompted my mother to let loose one of her favourite sayings. 'That's the straw that finally broke the camel's back!'

So, the poor creature had hardly put her paw over the threshold when my mother had begun to build a case against my having her. She then went all out to win her husband over to her side. Her main strategy was to call for a Vote. Voting was her favourite method of establishing anything new within the household, and she would lie to produce a two-to-one result in her favour. On this occasion, as my father was eating his dinner, she began weaving stories about Whiskers crapping everywhere. The poor cat seemed to be crapping so many times a day that her husband knew it was another of her preposterous inventions. Judging by the pitiful amount of food my mother dished up each day, it was impossible for Whiskers to litter the house in the way described. According to her, after Whiskers had littered "her" house she went outside and continued to litter "his" garden. If her husband wasn't paying attention to her ranting, which most of the time he wasn't, she knew that any mention of the word "garden" would rouse him from his ennui. He loved his garden more than he loved his wife.

Actually, my mother wouldn't have used the word "crapped". She would have said, "Did her business." She was unlikely to have known what "crap" meant, and if she did she would have pretended it didn't exist.

There were many things in her life that were never dwelt upon; "toilet functions" were one of them, although her obsession with cleanliness got her down on her knees to sanitise the toilet regularly. Swearing was totally forbidden in our house, and my father would receive untold reprimands if he used anything as strong as "damn," "devil" or even "blast". He hit his ankle with a spade once when he was turning the cabbage patch over and he screamed out a D-word. Although the man was in pain and there was blood staining his sock, my mother's only concern as she came dashing down the garden path was about his language.

Sandy Eccles was Mary's ginger tomcat. He didn't do me any favours in my struggle to keep Whiskers, because during the night he decided to find out more about his new female neighbour. Not having been castrated, his curiosity was unrestrained and his first act was to climb over the fence and spray objects near to our house. I had to agree with my mother: the odour was repugnant. Once again she repeated her "last straw" pronouncement, even though Whiskers wasn't the culprit.

Just eleven days after I had brought Whiskers home, I rushed home from school especially to be with her, only to find that the cardboard box in the yard where she had been sleeping was empty. She had been returned from whence she came, for no other reason than that she was a cat. I cried cups full of tears, but they didn't make any difference to my inveterate mother. I never saw Whiskers again. When my father arrived home from work that same evening, I looked to him for some understanding, but he was so under his wife's thumb it wouldn't have been worth his matrimonial alliance to argue against her. In the end, he promised to take me to watch Liverpool FC's next home fixture if I would only stop crying for five minutes.

Two weeks later, my mother informed me that poor little Whiskers had been hit by the number S2 Ribble bus outside the Co-op.

That put paid to my constant enquiries about her welfare. I was devastated almost beyond consolation, in the way most people are when they lose someone close.

Perhaps the only thing that got me through the sadness was the thought that Whiskers probably didn't have any regrets. If her life was to be spent in the chilly atmosphere of the Co-op food store or the frozen one under my mother's roof, where repression, persecution and discrimination reigned, then the poor little mite was probably better off out of it.

A month after my mother sent Whiskers back, I found out that she had been a useless ratter, which was why Bob Jackson had off-loaded her onto me. In the meantime, the Co-op had found a replacement for her, so they weren't best pleased when she was returned to them.

Whiskers

2 Lucy

Some thirty or so years on from the Whiskers episode, a second cat entered my life. For most of the intervening time I had been working as a stage designer and scenic artist in the British theatre, television and film world. This meant I had to travel a lot, so it wasn't possible for me to provide the settled situation that a cat or, for that matter, any pet needs. It was only when I left the entertainment business, bought a semi-detached house in a small town in Surrey and started my own business, painting Trompe l'Oeil murals in the homes of the well-to-do that I started to consider having a cat. What also encouraged the idea was that my partner, Nicola suggested that we should keep some animals.

When we met, Nicola was working as a legal secretary for a partnership of solicitors in nearby Godalming. In her spare time she was the secretary of the local soccer club I played for and one evening, after an away fixture we went out for a few drinks, which in due course led to our life-long relationship and eventual marriage. During our first year as an item, Nicola continued to live with her parents in nearby Witley, but she spent the majority of her weekends at my place. Before I met her I'd been quite happy living on my own, but around the first anniversary of our meeting she suggested that she move into my house on a permanent basis. She added that of course she would be prepared to pay me rent.

I'm sure Nicola knew I wouldn't turn down her proposal because she had already been moving in piecemeal, and I hadn't said or done anything to prevent it.

As an avid reader, Nicola has never been far away from a book, so consequently a growing collection of them had started to fill vacant spaces in my bookcase. I'd also noticed there were clothes hanging in my closet that weren't mine, and her wash things had begun to get mixed in with mine on the bathroom shelf. When I noticed a teddy bear had crept into what had become our bed (and it had brought its own pillow), it was just a matter of her bringing a couple more suitcases of clothes and a large box of shoes for the process to be complete.

One weekend of the third month from when Nicola had moved in, we'd noticed that a cat had started to peer at us through the glass panelled French doors that opened onto our back garden. It was grey with fawn bits, a tortoise shell back and a white front. We didn't know its name, its sex or where it came from, but our next-door neighbours told us it lived at number fifty-two, four doors down the street. They told us her name was Lucy and that she wasn't very happy in her current home, because her owners' behaviour had suddenly become upsetting for her. The more Lucy came to visit us the longer she began to stay, especially when we started to feed her. Consequently we soon became very fond of her, because Nicola is about as lovesick as it is possible to be over cats (or any animal, come to that), especially one that happened to be looking for a home. My house, in which I had lived alone for five years, was becoming more populated.

A couple of months after Lucy had begun visiting (and in the process of making her dietary likes and dislikes known to us), Nicola and I were sitting in the back garden enjoying some extraordinarily pleasant British weather when we heard the beginnings of a very loud commotion. It seemed to come four doors down the road and it involved two human voices, one female and one male, and they were going at it hammer and tongs. We could also hear objects going bump, bang and crash.

Judging by the number of net curtains that were being swished about along the street, we weren't the only ones paying an interest in the proceedings. The noise was soon followed by Lucy more or less flying over the adjoining fence and running into our house at top speed.

Two days later we heard an even bigger row, and while it was in full swing, Lucy again came running to us for shelter. It was then we realised there were serious matrimonial problems happening within earshot. Then the neighbour across the street told Nicola, in confidence that the marriage difficulty of the couple in number fifty-two was irreconcilable. A child's welfare should always be paramount if a matrimonial break-up is in an advanced stage and Lucy was their only child.

A few days later, the wife moved out, followed a few weeks after by the husband. In the meantime Lucy had already decided she preferred to live with us, amidst peace and quiet and massive amounts of love and harmony, so we spoke to the husband before he left, to make sure he was happy for us to adopt her. All we needed to know about Lucy was how old she was and whether she had been neutered. He told us he was happy for us to take care of her, that she was eight and that she had indeed been neutered. We were so pleased. Thankfully the husband seemed pleased, our neighbours next door and across the street seemed to be pleased, but best of all, Lucy seemed to be pleased that her life would be free of noise or flying household objects. And although she could not possibly have grasped the fact, she wasn't going to be torn in half in a custody battle.

Soon after that, we also moved. We needed more space, and with two salaries coming in we could afford to upgrade. Our choice of a new home was a pretty, 16th century three-bedroom Elizabethan Cottage with oak beams and a barn.

Building societies had recently announced they were keen to lend money to couples that weren't married, although we didn't need much of a joint mortgage to be able to take on the cottage. So, one day we asked Lucy if she would like to move house, with the prospect of her having her own bedroom and she said she would.

A couple of weeks after my house had been sold and we had moved to the cottage, Lucy didn't seem at all happy that she'd agreed to the move, because she started to scratch herself, so much so she began to look as if she was infected with the mange. Naturally we took her to the vet, who told us she was flea-ridden. He asked us if the previous owners of the cottage had pets and it turned out they had a dog, which had left most of his fleas behind in the fitted carpets we'd inherited. We had them all removed and had a man from the council spray the entire house and its contents with some sort of transparent liquid; the only things he didn't spray were Lucy and us. We then bought new carpets. Sure enough, Lucy stopped scratching and her fur began to grow again, filling her balding patches.

This was just one of many episodes that revealed our lack of experience as cat owners. Nicola's parents had always owned dogs, so having a cat was even more of a new experience for her than it was for me. Because my association with Whiskers was so brief and so long ago, I hadn't learnt much from it (nor did I remember any of it), so we bought several textbooks on cats in order to improve our parenting techniques. People had told us that cats are independent creatures that are quite capable of looking after themselves, but we found this to be as untrue as it was casual and half-hearted. Agreed, they don't need exercising like dogs do and they can be left alone in a house, providing they have access to the outside or to a litter tray, food and fresh water but, like a dog or any other pet, if a cat is domesticated it needs constant attention if it is to have a good life.

I firmly believe that people who think cats can be left to their own devices are not worthy of keeping them, and on several occasions I have made firm attempts to put such individuals right.

Lucy was a lovely, soft-natured cat and she appeared to be grateful for our adopting her. There might have been a language barrier, but that was easily overcome because there was a desire to communicate. We soon learnt that a cat could teach us a lot about life. The non-cat owner or the casual owner who doesn't make an intense study of their fellow creature is most definitely missing out. A cat is wise beyond belief. They are equipped with twice as many facilities to survive as humans. They are sensible, analytic, clever, sensitive and knowledgeable. They are determined, single-minded, protective, courageous, courteous, sane, comical, loving, beautiful and highly intelligent. They are enthusiastic about life, and that enthusiasm rubs off on their human companions. They can also be self-centred, envious, cunning and jealous. They are hostile, ruthless killers too, but we ignore that side of them – that is, until they bring home evidence to prove it.

For the next three years Nicola and I settled into our life together, always making sure that one of us was around to care for Lucy. We also made some additions to the family. The first was a rabbit. (I know this story is supposed to be about our cats, but please bear with me.) When we saw a newspaper advert offering a bunny for free in the nearby village of Albury, we went to collect him. He was a white Himalayan with black ears, a black tail and pink eyes. I built him a large cage and he settled into it well. He needed a name, so we called him after the village where we got him - Albury. Two weeks later Nicola saw two completely black rabbits, one male and one female for sale in a pet shop window. It was wintertime and as they were only a few weeks old, we kept them in the house in two more cages I had built.

In the evenings and at the weekends we would let them run around the house, and we would have a great time together. On fine days they would run around the garden, but we never let them out of our sight in case they went under a fence. Throughout their stay, Lucy seemed to enjoy their company, apart from when they became a bit too mischievous and tried to climb on her back.

One evening, when the rabbits were out of their cage, the fridge suddenly stopped working. Then, as we were watching television, that too went dead. When we went to investigate, we found the rabbits had eaten through two live electrical cables. I later found out that rabbits have insulated feet and can resist a single-phase mains electric current going through them. They are not resistant to a three-phase current, so from then on, as the cooker was three-phase, and as it was spring I put their cages outside next to Albury's in case one or both chewed through the cooker cable and blew themselves to bits.

Besides buying books on cat ownership, we also bought volumes on rabbit welfare. In one, it said that a rabbit is sexually mature when it reaches eight months old. Its advice on breeding rabbits was to be sure to introduce a male into the female's cage rather than the other way round, otherwise a serious fight will ensue. If this is done properly, mating will occur almost before the cage door has been closed. To see if this was so, I did as the book said. It turned out to be the case. It was instantaneous. And really I do mean instantaneous.

Four months later, our rabbit population had increased to nine, with six, absolutely gorgeous all-black babies appearing in the nesting box I had provided. They were all gorgeous. I then had to get busy making six more cages for them, as well as a long chicken-wire covered run in the garden so they could get some exercise. However, one of them seemed intent on leaving us and one afternoon dug a burrow three metres deep. If I hadn't managed to persuade him out of it he could have gone on digging for a long way.

The next day I stapled a chicken-wire base to the run, which inhibited his digging.

In the meantime Albury was nearly two-years-old and

still a male virgin, and he seemed to be getting extremely frustrated about being excluded from his fellows' baby-making capers. In his anxiety he had started to pull his fur out in great clumps. One of our rabbit books confirmed that this was through sexual deprivation, and so I let him loose with the mature black female for a day or two. The result was three more black babies, a few black-and-white ones and an all-white one. This brought the total up to fifteen in all, at which point Nicola put a stop to my experimentation, fearing that we would be overrun.

We found some good homes for four of them in nearby Guildford and two of Nicola's work colleagues took two more, but all the adopters expected cages to be provided with each rabbit or they wouldn't take them, so I was kept very busy paying the price for getting carried away with my breeding programme. There were other people who said they'd have some for their children, again on the proviso I made even more cages. So, in the end this brought our remaining head count down to five in all, who were from then on strictly segregated.

While all this was going on, Lucy hadn't been forgotten. This chapter is dedicated to her and her memory and not to our rabbits, cute as they were. Lucy wasn't the kind of cat who would let us forget her, and she would let us know loudly if we tried to do something without involving her. We still had a lot to learn about cats, and it was the stuff the books didn't mention, mainly because books generalise about cats' behavioural patterns and instincts. What they cannot possibly do is describe each cat's individual character and personality (perhaps that should be "catality"), because each one is entirely different and Lucy certainly had loads of "catality."

Lucy would respond to a whistle. This was also a surprise to us, because we imagined it was only dogs that came to heel when called, but if we hadn't seen her for a couple of hours or so, with my head poking out of a window a sharp whistle or two would alert her and bring her home. Sometimes she would bound back, all enthusiastic, but sometimes she would stroll nonchalantly back, only half-interested to find out what the commotion was all about. When I told her I'd been worried about her and I didn't like her wandering off too far, she would shrug her shoulders as if to say, 'shucks, don't be so silly.'

I fitted a cat flap to our back door to save us having to leave it permanently ajar. To do it I had to cut a circular hole eight inches above ground level, and as the building was five hundred years old and Grade 1 listed I guessed that planning permission was necessary to do this. I also guessed that more than likely it would have been denied. But as the cat flap was a necessity I went ahead and did it regardless. An inanimate object can easily be replaced, but a cat cannot. I found out later that not all cats would use a cat flap, because it's not a natural obstacle. Lucy balked at it at first, but with Nicola on the outside of the back door and me on the inside we soon persuaded her to get accustomed to it by gently passing her back and forth. She didn't seem to be confused by this additional architectural feature or protest at it and later that day, after we'd left her alone to figure it out, we heard her happily flapping it backwards and forwards without our assistance.

Like a lot of cats, Lucy was a pernickety eater. She wouldn't touch cheap brands and nor was she a big eater. At first I was concerned, because I thought cats ate more than she did. Lucy would ask for tinned food, but when it was presented to her she wouldn't touch it. Then, when she did decide to eat, she would insist on it being fresh. It could be meat or fish from a tin that had been opened and kept in the fridge for a day or two, but if there were remains left in her bowl from a previous feed she wouldn't touch that either, even if it had only been placed in her bowl an hour or so before. When it was time to eat, we had to provide a clean bowl with a dollop of fresh food in it every time. Trying to fool her by mixing new with old was an expensive mistake, because she wouldn't touch any of it. On several occasions Nicola tried to be firm with her by leaving it in the bowl for as long as it took, but she still refused. Instead, she would skirt around it every time and fill up on the biscuits. If we removed the biscuits as a way of forcing her to eat the tinned food she had left, she would go off in a huff until we gave in.

I went out one day, leaving Nicola at home. When I came back, she was not in a good mood. When I asked her what was wrong, she said she'd had a battle of wills with Lucy over food. Nicola was fed up with Lucy being so picky, so she had waited until she asked for food, hoping she'd be hungry enough to eat what she was given. But, when she presented Lucy with a bowl of food from the fridge that she' had refused earlier that morning; as soon as Lucy realised it was food she'd already left, she gave the bowl a derisory sniff and strolled into the lounge. Nicola had bought some exotic dried flowers and ferns, the type of modern, spread-out arrangement that doesn't come cheap. She'd arranged them in a large, expansive display in a basket and placed it on the lounge carpet. A short while later, Nicola followed Lucy into the lounge and noticed her new floral display was wet.

'At first I thought it was water,' Nicola said. 'But how could it have been? Then I gave it a sniff, because I suspected it might be something else. It was. I'm certain she peed on it as a deliberate gesture to demonstrate her disapproval.' Needless to say, the display was ruined and Nicola had to throw it out. Later when Nicola had cooled down, she said we'd been lucky that it was only dried flowers we'd lost. Maybe she could have chosen to burn the house down!

Feeding time for most animals in the wild is at sunrise and at sunset, but of course if there is food to be had between hours, then so much the better. Domestic cats know instinctively when it's time to wake up, which is usually twenty minutes before their humans' alarm is due to go off. Being woken at five in the morning by Lucy so we could have the pleasure of serving her fresh cat food could be a bit of a bind, especially at weekends when neither Nicola nor I were working. Being forced to walk down three flights of stairs to get to the kitchen when half asleep was never easy. Mercifully, during the week Nicola got up at six each morning to get ready for work, so on occasions Lucy would grant me a lie in. (By the way, seasonal time changes mean nothing to a cat. They have an in-built clock and know when it's five o'clock.)

To get me to feed her Lucy would employ various methods to wake me at five. One of them was to jump on me from the top of a chest of drawers. She would then walk all over me several times, and if I hadn't stirred by then she would tickle my face with her whiskers. If I refused to let this work, her second method (and her most successful) was to lie on my chest with her nose pressed against mine and breathe into my nostrils, all the time looking intently at my eyes until she saw a chink of reflected light. When she did, she knew her mission had been a success. I would put up as much resistance as I could by turning my face away so I could continue sleeping, but she would remain insistent. I'm sure cats' whiskers are the tickliest things on earth. At least they are for me, and once I've been tickled I cannot stop myself scratching. Why she always chose to torment me and not Nicola I never found out, mainly because five o'clock in the morning was never the hour to discuss the matter.

The most alarming method she employed to get me out of bed only happened once. As she was lying on my chest, breathing into my nostrils and peering at my eyes (on this occasion I was awake, but pretending to be asleep), she lifted my eyelid up with a single claw.

I nearly freaked, but I did not dare move. I lay there, rigid. I prayed she would let go and eventually she did. Before that, even if she had been successful in waking me, I would keep my eyes closed in the hope she'd get fed up and go away. But on this particular weekend morning, she decided to call my bluff and put an end to my stubbornness forever. For a moment or two with my arms and hands underneath the bed clothes I was completely at her mercy, but thankfully she had the good sense to let go.

In 1990, three years after we'd moved into the cottage, the financial recession fell upon us. For Nicola, work at the solicitor's office was still steady, but for how long would it last? For me the question had already been answered. I was finding it tough to keep going. In times of financial adversity, commissions for artwork can dry up literally overnight. I'd experienced two financial downturns already and I didn't fancy having to withstand a third. With this latest one, even the very wealthy had started to feel the pinch and had drawn in their horns. When Nicola and I first met, and before Lucy arrived on the scene, we had been to Spain and had a wonderful and memorable holiday touring the country. I liked the look of an old mountaintop village near Seville called Arcos de la Frontera, and I had said to Nicola at the time how I fancied living in an aesthetically satisfying place where every day brings joy to the soul. This recession seemed to be the appropriate time to make the move, mainly because during the previous one I had nearly gone under and the present one wasn't looking any brighter. Therefore I hoped that by the time the next one arrived I wouldn't be around to feel its effect.

In the end (or perhaps it was the beginning), we started to make firm plans to emigrate, but it wouldn't be to Spain. When Nicola was a teenager, she had been an au pair for an Italian family. This was in a little village called Moltrasio on the western shore of Lake Como, and in the two years she had been in their employment they had formed a friendship that continued long after

Nicola returned to England. She kept in touch by telephone with Elaine (the mother of the family), and during one particular conversation, Nicola told Elaine we were about to transfer ourselves to Spain. 'What a coincidence,' Elaine had said. 'We're also about to move.

My husband has had his office transferred to Rome, and we leave Moltrasio next month!'

So, after a twenty-minute phone conversation with Elaine, our Spanish plan was changed to an Italian one. We would rent her family home, and the rent wouldn't be very much because Elaine was pleased to have somebody she knew looking after her house.

Within three weeks of that conversation, we had found tenants for our house in Godalming. A couple of friends had said they were interested in renting it for a year, or maybe longer, which was fine with us because we didn't know if our adventure would work out, and we might have to come back after a year. After that, all we had to do was find a good home for Lucy, send some of our heavier things to Italy by road transport, pack a couple of bags, and catch a plane to Milan.

If this all sounds off-hand (and indeed it might), it isn't; and it wasn't easy, because Lucy's welfare was at stake. We spent hours discussing whether to take her with us, and twice we nearly cancelled the trip at the thought of having to leave her behind. Our main concern now was not the encroaching recession, but Lucy. Although our intentions of finding a more satisfying place to live were firmly rooted, the recession was only about money and things would pick up; but if it hadn't been for Nicola's sister Rose in Rugby (who was as much a cat lover as us), who promised to give Lucy a good home, we would have delayed or even abandoned the whole idea. In the end it did work out, and when we phoned Rose from Italy to check how Lucy was getting on, Rose told us Lucy was exploring her new home, eating well (only fresh food, of course), and didn't appear to be missing us at all.

This was a relief to hear but at the same time it made us disconsolate, because we were certainly missing her. In our hearts we wanted to be reunited with her, but for her sake we knew it wasn't to be.

Lucy

3 Uli

As well as wanting to escape the recession in the UK, we went to Italy because we like the ambience of the country, especially that of the medieval villages. We felt the same about some of the older villages in England, but having lived in a few of those we wanted to sample what village life was like abroad and to immerse ourselves in a different culture. Some people say it takes great courage to swap countries - especially when one of those making the change doesn't speak a word of that country's language! Nicola's Italian was fluent even then, but my Italian was virtually non-existent, nevertheless, we were looking forward to the challenge and because Nicola had already lived in Italy and knew the country well enough and I had holidayed in northern and central Italy on two other occasions, we were convinced that the country was worth making the effort for.

Others do not always understand the reasons why Brits emigrate, thinking of them as idlers, boozers or tax evaders. We fitted none of those categories. We left with no strings attached and arrived as straight (and possibly naïve) foreigners, with no insurance, no guarantees and no jobs. We wanted to earn our keep in Italy, so took a chance and trusted in luck. The only thing we had to fall back on if we failed to stay the course was the house we owned in Godalming.

This was our plan, but we only had enough money to tide us over for a year so if we didn't find work, we'd have to come back home. Nicola had said before we left England that if necessary she was prepared to do anything to enable us to survive, in the hope that later on she might be able to find something to which she was better suited.

However, within only six weeks our work concerns were alleviated. One afternoon, as I was lying on a sun-lounger in the garden of our new home, soaking up the heat of a June day, I received a telephone call. It was from a couple that had just bought a newly converted apartment in a magnificent neoclassical villa Taverna on the Eastern side of the lake and they wanted me to paint murals on some of the walls.

This particular villa is set in the ancient village of Torno, directly across the lake from Moltrasio. A landmark, and one of the largest and most harmonious pieces of architecture in the area, it was built by the Tanzi family in the mid-eighteenth century and is set in a magnificent private park. It was enlarged by the Taverna family some years later when they gave it both an open, rectangular look and their name. When the last of the Taverna family passed away in the early 1980s, the villa was sold to a property developer, who converted it into ten large luxury apartments.

We made an appointment to meet the client at their apartment and they commissioned me to do two Trompe l'Oeil murals, one in the lounge and the other in their dining room and apply matching colour washes to the remaining walls. They also wanted an extensive amount of oil-based paint effects applied to their internal doors and to the several pairs of French windows that led to their terraced garden. They added that they would be away on holiday for the whole of July and August, so I took this period as an opportunity to get most of the work done. This was good timing, because the paint effects to the internal doors and the French windows meant they needed to be left open for several days and nights to dry properly. Also, because there was a lot of work to do I reckoned that I would need an assistant to do the preparation work whilst I did the artwork and I had just the person in mind.

Up until I began work on the mural, Nicola had not painted a door, a window frame or a wall in her life. But because she is both extremely bright and hard working, I only needed to show her once how to do the preparation work required, and she carried it out to perfection. She was good at covering the furniture and the floors with plastic and cotton dust sheets, and masking the electrical fittings with newspaper and tape. She became good at washing the brushes, buckets and rollers after she had finished using them. She was also good at making lunch.

Although the villa is located on the opposite side of the lake, travelling to and from it was easy as public ferryboats criss-cross the lake all day. Our journey across to Torno passed through a stretch of the lake that offers one of the most exhilarating views in the world. From the terminal we had a longish walk through the village, eventually arriving at a set of impressive, automatic-opening, wrought iron gates with gold finials. To get to the main house, we had to walk through the extensive and stunning garden. In or around one of the six greenhouses we would regularly see Signor Gino, the head gardener. He seemed part of the fabric of the place and I don't think I would have been surprised if somebody had told me he had been there since the 1800's. An upright, good-hearted man, he was well into his eighties and the type of elegant person one might read about in a romantic historical novel. His hands were large, rough in texture and grey in colour; and the first time he shook mine it looked as though he was handing me some kind of root vegetable he'd just pulled up.

As we got to know each other better, he would often accompany us through the part of the estate that led to the apartment, to see how the murals were progressing. As we walked, he would recount stories of when he first started work as a boy on the estate seventy years earlier, and how he had witnessed a lot of changes to the villa, especially since it had been bought by a property developer and converted into modernised apartments.

He also recalled the 1950's, when the Contessa Taverna used to sit looking out of the dining room window overlooking the south garden - the very room we were painting. He said the room had always been *latte bianco* (milk white) in colour and without decoration, but he was sure she would have approved of the murals.

On the twenty-first day of our work schedule, as we approached the back door to the apartment we saw, propped against the doorstep and in the full glare of the early morning sun a tiny baby bird. It was squawking at the top of its voice, which risked attracting any of the feral cats that we had seen roaming the nearby woods. I picked it up immediately. Where this little bundle of grey and brown fluff had come from was a mystery. There were hundreds of magnificent trees on the estate, but there were none in the vicinity of the back door and there was no sign of a parent bird anywhere.

Another mystery was that it was late in the year to find a wild baby bird. We took it into the kitchen and placed it on the granite work surface. I poured some long-life milk into a saucer, but the bird just stared at it. Nicola found a pipette in a bathroom cabinet, filled it with milk, touched the end of it on the little bird's beak until it opened wide, then squeezed a few drops into its mouth. I scratched around a bit further and found some stale bread in the pantry. Nicola broke it into minute pieces, soaked it in the milk to soften it and then fed it to the bird. Suddenly the tiny creature became enthusiastic, and within a few seconds we discovered what a ferocious appetite it had. This meant that the rest of our day was taken up with a small amount of painting and a large amount of feeding.

Before we set out for work that day, we certainly hadn't expected to be rooting around in somebody else's fridge to find different foodstuffs to chop up to feed a half-starved bird. After the bread and milk, we tried bits of smoked Parma ham and sweetcorn, on which the little bird seemed to be particularly keen, but after three feeds in an hour he got fed up with it. We then tried bits of Ferrero Rocher chocolate dipped in orange juice, which got him interested.

Whether or not we were doing the right thing by feeding a baby bird such food, we didn't know. Are baby birds carnivores, omnivores or veggies? There wasn't time to delve into the matter. We had a starving bundle of feathers that wasn't interested either way. Nicola said his own body would tell him what he wanted to eat, but we didn't want to destroy his metabolism and nor did we want to see him fade away, so we gave him plenty of choice.

When Signor Gino visited us later that day for a chat, we showed him the baby bird and we asked him if he knew what sort it might be. He said it was a sparrow, and that it wouldn't survive for longer than a couple of days, because it would die from the shock of being handled by humans.

That evening we caught the boat back to Moltrasio, carrying our new friend in a cardboard box (into which we had punched some air holes). Back home, we continued the feeding process with a selection of foods that we thought would be more appropriate (and healthier), in the hope that our "sparrow" would survive.

In the meantime we named him (we'd already decided it was male) Uli, which we took from the Italian *uccellino*, meaning baby bird. On the veranda leading to the back garden, we had seen an elaborate Victorian cane birdcage that Elaine had left behind, so we brought it into the kitchen and placed Uli in it. That way he was able to watch us cook and eat our evening meal, and at the same time we could give him various tit-bits. Then, after our and his feeding process was over, we transferred the cage (including Uli) to the lounge, where we could watch the television together. This seemed agreeable to him.

At around ten o'clock, Nicola placed a cover over his cage and we went to bed. We hoped to sleep until six o'clock, but Uli had other ideas and at five he began demanding his breakfast.

The pipette we had borrowed was working overtime, being filled and refilled with water or milk. To try and imitate a parent bird's beak, we used a cocktail stick to push morsels of food down Uli's gullet. We soon learned from experience that we had to feed him to capacity at every sitting, so that he would cease squawking for at least a few minutes. Then, one of us would place him back in his cage so he could have a further sleep. He preferred to be placed on the floor of the cage, because his feet were not large enough or strong enough to grip the perch. Uli was also happy waddling around the kitchen table or whatever flat surface we placed him on, but the cage was useful because putting him in it prevented our living area from becoming one large toilet.

For the first three weeks we had Uli we had to abandon him during the day, because we still hadn't finished the work at the villa across the lake. When we returned in the evenings we could hear his shrill racket from thirty metres away, and that was with all the windows closed. Then we would feed him until he could hardly move. Signor Gino's prediction that he wouldn't survive more than a few days was proving to be wrong. Instead he became even more demanding, but he was so very cheeky and full of character and mischief that we started to fall in love with him. After two more weeks, there was enough definition in his tail and wing feathers to work out that he wasn't a sparrow, because his plumage was beginning to turn from a fuzzy grey and brown into a distinctive black and white. It was time to consult Archibald Thorburn's coloured illustrations of European birds. At this stage in Uli's growth it was still unclear as to what he was, but according to three of Thorburn's illustrations he could be a pied flycatcher, a crested tit or possibly a lesser whitethroat. Whatever Uli was, he was turning into a little beauty. What he most certainly wasn't, was a sparrow.

When his plumage had grown to what we thought was a sufficient amount, we started giving him flying lessons.

I would perch him on my finger, then without giving him any warning I would suddenly drop my arm down, causing him to flap his wings so he could retain his balance. The intention of this exercise was to strengthen the wing muscles and ligaments he needed to sustain flight. At first, he didn't bother to try. He had two humans who did all his flying around for him, providing the fifteen square meals a day he demanded. This resulted in him being overfed, with his midriff too big in relation to his wingspan. That was going to make flying, which he was almost ready for, that much more difficult. One evening, as he was sitting on top of my head (the position he had adopted while I watched television in the lounge), I felt him grip my scalp with both his feet. He then fluttered his wings and flew for the first time. This was no more than a few metres, but at least we had lift-off. He seemed to be aiming for the curtain rail, but to our surprise - then to our horror - he didn't quite make it. He crashed into the wall, slithered down it and hit the marble floor with an unpleasant, feathery thud. It seemed as if he not only demanded food when he wanted it, he also demanded attention.

After we had finished the Torno job we had more time to spend with Uli, especially during the day. We enjoyed his company very much, and he seemed to like ours - for whenever we swapped rooms he would insist on coming with us, perched either on a forefinger, a shoulder or a head. If I were painting at a table or easel, he would perch on the edge of an open paint can, content to watch me for hours. He had become as attached to me as I had to him.

At the end of his sixth week with us, his black and white feathers were almost fully developed. He had slimmed down a good deal and was in beautiful condition. His flying skills were developing nicely; his take-offs were fine, and although his landings still suffered the occasional miscalculation, Nicola made me realise that it was time for him to stretch his wings in preparation for him leaving the nest. 'We don't want him to go,' she said, 'but we should start thinking about introducing him to the wild. It isn't fair to keep him locked in the house any longer.'

The painful moment had arrived when we had to say goodbye, and we tried to prepare ourselves for what we expected to be an emotional farewell. I carried Uli into the garden, where there were enough overhanging trees for him to practice taking off and landing. Should he fall, the lawn would give him a soft landing. However, Uli wasn't going to do things by halves. He seemed to be eyeing up some large palm trees in the neighbour's garden on the opposite side of Via Regina, the main road that follows the western edge of Lake Como. So, with him on the end of my index finger I turned to face the palm trees. He walked up and down my finger a couple of times, crouched down as if to count to three and leapt into the air. He flew about two metres and landed inside a small bush low to the ground. I fished him out of it and we prepared to try once again. After he'd brushed himself down and regained some composure he made another one-two-three count and took off again, as anticipated, towards the neighbour's palm trees. This time he made it over the bush and over the railings that surrounded the garden, but instead of making it to the palm trees he fell short, crash-landing in the middle of the main road. Panic set in with us like you wouldn't believe. It couldn't have been a worse place to land. As fast as my legs would carry me, I flew down the three flights of stairs that led to the road, managed to unlock a door in the surrounding wall and scooped him up in my hand, before any vehicle came along and squashed him. That was enough trauma for me for one day. I locked him back in his cage. He wasn't yet up to it, so saying goodbye could wait for another day.

The following day we tried again. He still seemed intent on the hard route to the palm trees, so this time Nicola decided to stand in the middle of the road, ready to flag down any passing traffic should he not make it all the way. Uli seemed to know when she was in place, and after yet another one-two-three count (he was getting good at that part) he made a long, low swoop over the road, rising up to make a nice professional landing in the dense foliage. When Nicola returned to the garden, we stood there looking at him as he looked back at us. Feeling forlorn, we waved a tearful goodbye to him. He looked so sweet; a tiny black and white dot in a mass of green leaves. It was the furthest he had been away from us in the six weeks he'd been with us. Then we waited for him to fly off into the big, blue beyond. But nothing happened.

Instead, we looked at one another for about fifteen minutes and then he took off, hovered over the palms, and came straight back and landed on the top of my head, where he received more kisses and cuddles than any bird has ever received in its lifetime. We fully expected him to take off again after a brief rest - but no, he seemed content to return indoors for something to eat and drink.

It was now the height of summer and temperatures were well over the thirty-degree mark. This meant that all the windows to every room needed to be left wide open day and night to receive the maximum amount of through draught we needed to remain cool. This new freedom to move wherever he liked suited Uli perfectly. He could fly in and out, over and round the house at random and without abandoning us. From the time we'd adopted him I had talked and whistled gently in his ear, so that he knew to associate certain sounds with food and stroking. Now he had started going out, all I had to do was whistle or call him and without hesitation, he would arrive and land on my head or forefinger in anticipation of being fed or stroked. People could hear my whistle up to forty metres away, but Uli could hear it at treble that distance.

By now, we were fairly sure he was a pied flycatcher, which is a breed people do not keep in captivity.

We had told our new friends, Enzo and Ada about Uli and how remarkable he was, and they were eager to meet him. We organised a lunch date, so we could introduce him to them and have him demonstrate his flying skills. When he did, they could hardly believe what they saw. This occasion became very memorable for us. We were eating salad on the veranda, and when I whistled for Uli to begin his performance, he came whizzing over our heads and landed on the rim of Enzo's plate. He then started to eat Enzo's salad, at the same time allowing Enzo, a complete stranger to him to stroke his back. Then he hopped from plate to plate, pecking at bread, tossing bits of grated carrot into the air or standing on the brim of our glasses, drinking the contents. He finished his display by flying to the side table and taking a vigorous bath in his drinking water, splashing it all over us. It was wonderful to watch.

Sometimes, Uli would demonstrate how spoiled and short-tempered he had become in his quest for attention, particularly if I was painting something he regarded as taking too long to finish when he felt I should be spending my time with him and not on earning a living. I could be standing at my easel, applying paint to canvas with a long-handled brush, and if we hadn't had any contact for an hour or so he would arrive at top speed, slowing down from around fifty kilometres an hour to zero within a metre, to land on the ideal perch – my paintbrush. Then he would edge along the brush handle to the bristle end and start attacking it with real purpose. Once, Nicola took a photograph of him in the process of wrecking a number eight Chinese hog's-hair brush, whilst getting his beak and head covered in emerald green acrylic paint.

One day, my whistle lost its magic and he failed to appear. He had, it seemed, chosen to fly out of earshot. It had been around three months since we first found him on the doorstep to the Villa Taverna, and the day of his departure had come.

We hoped and prayed it was a momentary glitch and that he would return, but after a week of my walking up and down his regular flight path, straining and whistling until I was dry, I finally had to admit that the call of the wild was too strong.

For a long time after that, if I saw a pied flycatcher in the garden (or even when I was in the car), I would stop and try my famous call with as much gusto and love as I could muster, but there was never a response. Three months is but the blink of an eye in the great expanse of time, but if an emotional relationship has been forged and it is broken - then boy, does it hurt.

4 New Surroundings

Three years later, Nicola and I were still working and we were still solvent. I was receiving a satisfactory number of mural commissions and she had found a secretarial post in Milan. Then things changed, when Elaine called to tell us that she and her husband needed to sell their house to enable them to put their son and daughter through university in Rome. On asking around, we found a small apartment to rent in the Piazza Recchi, which is in the *centro storico* (historical centre) of Moltrasio. It was a picturesque setting, with a waterfall in the north-east corner of the piazza. The apartment was above a disused butcher's shop in a three-hundred-year-old building. Its front door opened directly onto a set of narrow stone steps that led up to the village. It was small and unfurnished, with only one bedroom. For how long it had been empty, we didn't know, but we reckoned it hadn't seen a paintbrush for a long time. There was no central heating and no gas and a stone sink with a single cold water tap hung loosely from the kitchen wall. After living in a four-storey, three-bedroom detached property with two gardens and all mod cons we would certainly have some adjusting to do, and it left us thinking for a while. But property prices had begun to climb dramatically and it turned out to be the only place we could find in Moltrasio that we could afford. We decided to ask the landlady if we could come to an arrangement over the living conditions. We wanted her to pay a plumber to connect the gas, put in a boiler and central heating, and replace the stone sink with a modern sink unit.

She agreed to pay for the installation of the boiler and

the new sink, leaving us to pay for the installation of the central heating and the radiators.

In the three years we had been in Italy I had accumulated a pile of art materials and associated equipment, and it was clear from the start that there was no room in our new apartment to store it. Nor was there space for me to produce any paintings, so I needed to find a studio with a storeroom. It seemed like a stroke of luck that soon after we moved into the apartment, the old butcher's shop below, which had been closed for thirty-seven years became available to rent, so I asked the landlady if she was prepared to let me have it. She was, and we struck a deal. Having a shop literally downstairs was very convenient, because it meant I could open its doors to display my work for sale to passing tourists.

Moltrasio is situated in a man-made valley on the western side of Lake Como, nine kilometres north of Como city centre. First recorded as the Roman settlement of Monteraso (meaning "shaved mountain"), it is famous for a very hard, dark grey, almost black stone, which was split into slabs to be used as steps, flooring and paving. The valley emerged as this stone was quarried. The village centre, at 250 metres above sea level, rests under the shadow of Monte Bisbino; from its summit, one can see more or less the entire Swiss Alps. It is without doubt one of the most spectacular views anywhere.

Most of the buildings in the centro storico are around three-hundred years old and are all built in the same style, with thick rendered stone walls, overhanging eaves and low pitched roofs covered in half-round terra cotta *tegole* (roof tiles). The rooms inside the houses are small, no larger than four by five metres but they have high ceilings, some covered in moulded plaster relief. The floors will be tiled in either ceramic or marble, and all the steps inside and out will be in the local black stone.

Most of the houses are narrow and high because, to lay

foundations, the bedrock had to be levelled by hand. Thus building land came at a premium. The lanes and passageways between the houses were narrow; built just wide enough to allow the passage of a laden mule. The view from outside the Church of San Martino is of a patchwork pattern of terra cotta roofs, golden ochre walls and dark forest green shutters, bordered by the dense trees that envelop the mountains and the lake beyond. In my view, it is without doubt one of man's better achievements in this modern world.

At home in our new surroundings, we soon discovered that the piazza outside our front door was a haven for a large population of feral cats. We had moved there in the early spring, which of course is the height of the mating season for the little darlings and outside our bedroom window, the cats' chorus was becoming extremely loud. Something had to be done if we were to get a good night's sleep. A head count revealed ten resident feral cats in the immediate proximity of our home, but with the mating season in full swing the scent of the females attracted quite a few more males. This influx caused some mighty bust-ups, with injuries being sustained during the fighting. Naturally, after a few more weeks we noticed that one of the females, a brown tabby was becoming rounder by the day, which made us very alarmed because we knew that this would yield lots of furry kittens - to which I have to confess that Nicola and I are suckers for. Sure enough, a few weeks later the tabby walked past our front door looking very much slimmer. This only meant one thing, that in six to eight weeks' time we could expect to see mum out for a walk, showing off her latest litter.

One morning in early July I heard the same mother cat bleating more than usual, so I went outside to the piazza to see what was wrong. I followed her gaze down the road and saw a tiny black-and-white kitten struggling to make it up the slope towards her, as if it were pulling a ton weight.

I slowly approached it and although it tried his best to

scamper away, I easily caught it and picked it up. It was one of the most gorgeous kittens imaginable, with a coat as soft and as shiny as silk. It had a black hood over a white face and a lovely pink nose. It was a real beauty. It was also very wet, possibly because it had just waded through the stream at the bottom of the waterfall near to where it had been born. On inspecting it, I discovered that it was a male and I also saw why he had been unable to walk properly: his intestine was hanging out of a large hole near his groin. By now his mother was giving me real grief, but when I offered her kitten back she ran off in the opposite direction, leaving me literally holding the baby. It was if she had been looking for a surrogate parent for her suffering baby. Now she had found one, her job was done.

Later that same day, when Nicola returned from Milan the first thing she saw were tiny paw prints on our apartment floor, left from the kitten's still-wet paws; she knew before she saw me that I had fallen in love while she had been at work. An hour later we were inside the vet's surgery in the next village, where he told us he didn't think there was much chance that the kitten would survive, as the hole was massive in proportion to the size of his body and he didn't know if he could stretch the skin across the gaping wound, but he would give it a try. While we were in his surgery he found a dog's tooth inside the hole, which explained what had happened.

After that, we telephoned the vet's secretary every few days to see what progress the kitten was making. He seemed to be surviving, and two weeks' later we went back to collect him. The vet told us the kitten had clung onto life beyond all expectation. With that, his future was sealed. We had found a replacement for Lucy, the cat we'd had to leave behind in England. We had said we would never take on the responsibility of having another animal, but knew in our heart of hearts we probably would.

Some time after, a sleek, white feral cat that roamed the

piazza regularly was seen to be putting on a kilo or more around her belly. A few weeks' later, she too passed by the studio looking her svelte self again. Six weeks later, right on cue she began parading four kittens around the piazza. Neighbours began throwing their hands up in horror at the sight of more kittens, becoming agitated at the thought of having to clean up the mess from their gardens. The animals would have to be poisoned before they became much older, they told us. We were horrified to hear this and promptly adopted three more kittens, as well as taking on the feeding of the rest of them.

We came to discover that only a small percentage of the Italian population look after their pets properly. Cats are generally treated like vermin. Dogs fare slightly better, but there are still too many residents who have the wrong motive for owning a dog, and a lot of them regard them as guard dogs first and as pets a very poor second. In the cities, dogs are often treated as fashion items. A few years ago the English setter was in vogue; then, it was good to be seen on the streets of Milan with a husky, or a collie or a shih-tzu. The question is: what happens to these dogs once that particular breed goes out of fashion? Dogs are also used to display their owner's wealth, paraded behind the big gates of smart villas. This is supposed to indicate to the passer-by that the owner must be rich and has something worth guarding. And in general, the higher the gates, the larger the dog (or dogs), telling any burglar on reconnaissance that if he fancies any of the prize possessions to be had, he risks getting ripped to pieces.

It is not in a cat's nature to guard anything belonging to another; therefore they are low in the Italians' estimation. 'What is the use of a cat, or any other animal,' they say. 'If it cannot earn its keep?'

Then the same people will add, 'of course some of them do catch rats, and cats are also good to eat.'

The first time we heard the last part of this statement

we thought we were mistaken; but then on another occasion we heard a neighbour expounding on the gastronomic delights of eating cat with polenta, and how she and many of the locals appreciate a plump cat roasted on a spit over a log fire. According to them, a cat served with polenta, the local maize dish makes a very tasty meal, especially on a cold winter's night. It began to dawn on us that they, or at least some of them, really do eat cats. I think our neighbour must have thought that when we said we were cat lovers, she thought we too enjoyed eating them. It had never entered her mind that somebody should want to keep a cat (or in our case, cats) as a pet; feeding it solely so that it can have a nice life, rather than fattening it up to be eaten at a later date. To her way of thinking (and many like her), anybody who spends good money on feeding an animal for no practical purpose must be insane.

It is important to understand that after the Roman Empire collapsed, the ordinary people of Italy suffered countless invasions and occupations of their country. This happened most recently during the Second World War, when the Nazis took control of Italy after the fall of Mussolini. Many Italians were subjected to both chronic hunger and poverty, so they ate whatever they could find. Cats were a source of fresh meat, so if there were a cat to be had, it would quickly end up on the dinner table. There are, at the time of writing, a few of those people left alive who had suffered directly under the hands of the Nazis. To some of them, the memory of that brutal time is as vivid as if it had happened yesterday. But to Nicola and me, it seems a peculiarity that in times of plenty a few of this older generation still like to eat cats - and are not too fussed whether they are feral or somebody's pet.

One night a group of us went to a trattoria, high in the mountains on the east side of the lake, and when the owner presented us with the menu, it read: "*gatto con polenta*" (cat with polenta). According to one member of our group, customers can bring in a cat of their choice the day before they've booked a table; and the chef will prepare, cook, and serve it, with piping hot polenta.

After one more pregnant female gave birth in our landlady's garden, it brought the headcount to twenty ferals. It was plain for anybody to see, that the man from the council would be brought round to lay his poison if people started to complain about the amount of cat poo they were having to contend with. This was when Nicola decided to take control of a worsening situation, and set out to have them all sterilised. With the patience of a saint and the aid of a few tins of Whiskas, she gradually gained the confidence of our feline neighbours. She would sit for hours at the foot of the stairs of our apartment, with the front door wide open and a bowl of fresh cat meat at the ready; coaxing nervous, always wary, often completely wild beasts to come closer and closer a little more each day. At first, there was no success at all while she was sitting near them. Of course, as soon as she moved away they all ran to the bowl and gobbled the food up Gradually she gained their confidence one by one, ingeniously using the evening breeze from the mountains to blow the irresistible smell of the food in the direction of the poor, skinny creatures, who could not resist the temptation any further and began to let her touch them as they were eating. Then, as calmly as possible, she would pick one up and slip it into the cat basket before it realised what had happened. She would then summon me from the sofa (where I was sitting quite comfortably, usually watching the football), telling me to fetch the car and rush our captive to the vet for sterilisation.

Nicola managed to capture all twenty ferals, which was an amazing achievement and at some considerable financial cost. The next part of her programme, which was as difficult as catching the cats, was to educate our human neighbours and to make sure they understood the efforts and expense she had been exerting in taking control of their and our responsibilities. This was all news to them, and most weren't interested at all when she told them that she had done something positive to resolve a problem that should have been sorted out years earlier. Some gave her verbal support, but they never offered any financial assistance. She knew they didn't really understand why she was doing what she was doing, and they probably wondered why she kept banging on about animal welfare, persistently telling them that it was everybody's responsibility to take care of them properly and not to go putting poison down as a cheap, short-term solution to a long-term problem.

After that, we made sure our official cats were looked after as well as, if not better than we looked after ourselves. They were well fed and happy, and they received the best medical attention money could buy. Sandro, the mobile vet, visited them regularly on his cross-country motorbike to administer check-ups. Our neighbours were happy in the knowledge that the remaining feral cats in the area had all been neutered, so the problem was unlikely to happen again. In the summertime, all our cats lay on the window sill of my art studio overlooking the piazza, basking in the sun; and more than one person said that they were a picture fit to paint.

So now let me tell you how we came to adopt what we term our 'official cats' that were once feral cats and I will start with the first. And he was the tiny kitten with the awful injury.

The Piazza Recchi Feral Cats

5 Roger's Black Pearls

The name we chose for the tiny, black-and-white baby with the mended hole in his stomach was Roger. He was the first cat we adopted in Italy and I'll tell you why we chose this rather simple name later on, but first of all let me tell you that Roger was wise, even when he was young. There was no kidding him; we were convinced he could read minds, especially mine. If Nicola and I were having a conversation, we would have to spell out the words we didn't want him to understand. If he picked up the thread of what we were talking about and he didn't like it, he would become very upset and give us a hard time. On the other hand - or perhaps it should be the other paw - if what he heard was to his liking, he could become very excited.

And he was skilful. Taking the lids off tins was pretty much the only thing Roger couldn't do. He was a chicken fiend, be it raw, cooked, or in a tin. He was also bilingual. If Nicola and I were having a discussion about food shopping, we always had to remember to spell out C-H-I-C-K-E-N or P-O-L-L-O, or write it down. But if (as we were sure) he could read minds, there wasn't much hope of any peace - if chicken was in the offing - until he'd had his fair share of it. Nor could he be fooled or fobbed off. If there was chicken in the house he would be aware of it the second it arrived and he could even smell it if it was wrapped in four layers of plastic and shut in the freezer. He would prepare himself to wait for his share of it, for days if necessary. Then, when we did get around to de-frosting it he would look at us with his disgusted look that said 'it's about ****** time.'

His passion for chicken must have begun when we got him home from the vet, after he had been successfully sewn back together. The first thing we gave him was cooked chicken; and it must have been the first time he had tasted it. We then tucked him into a woollen blanket, which must have been the first time he had ever felt the warmth of one. We put him on the divan in the lounge so he could have a good sleep, which is what he did. A few hours later it was our bedtime, and we made sure the door was ajar so Roger could wander in during the night if he felt up to it. Of course we checked on him several times during the night to see if he was all right, and he appeared to be sleeping like the baby he was. The next morning, he seemed to be getting used to his new surroundings. We hoped for a long relationship, and an hour into it we seemed to be getting on fine. Paradoxically though, half an hour later we couldn't find him anywhere - and I mean anywhere. In our small, fifty-five square metre apartment he had somehow vanished. We were staggered.

We looked inside and under everything we had, which wasn't a great deal. It wasn't possible to pack a great deal in an apartment of that size, and it took the two of us no more than fifteen minutes to look through everything we owned; some of it twice over. Nicola said she wasn't convinced I had looked through my things properly. When I complained that I had, she pushed me to one side and with no qualms began pulling my stuff out of my drawers, spreading it out on the floor. But still we couldn't find him. A few objects like missing earrings, hair grips and an assortment of pens, pencils and coins came to light, but no kitten. Then we realised our bedroom window had been left wide open, and there was a five-metre drop from it onto the stone pathway that led to our landlady's garden.

Together we peered through the window.

'He wouldn't have, would he?' We both asked.

'Surely he hasn't jumped. It's too high for him, isn't it?'

'He can't have. Or can he?'

'I think he must have done!'

Suddenly we both decided that jumping out of the window was the only way he could have got out of the apartment. Yet we couldn't accept that we had lost him. It was inconceivable. He was so sweet and we felt so sick. We wanted to give him the world, so why had he wanted to leave us? 'Please, God, return him to us...' Then the panic set in.

Two weeks at the vet and a small fortune in charges to save the little darling's life, and he wanted to leave us. How, we wanted to know could such a tiny creature, especially one with twenty stitches holding a severe wound together survive a fall from such a height. It was an anguishing thought to say the least. We knew cats to be resilient, but not from the effects of falling from a height like that. There was no time to lose. He must be suffering somewhere. So we went next door to ask - no, to beg - our landlady to let us in, so we could search her garden for him. We pressed the intercom button on the wall beside her monolithic iron gates and we waited.

We pressed again, and waited. I pressed my ear against the speaker. We pressed again, but still there was nothing. Perhaps it wasn't working; that would often be the case with old electrical wiring. But it was half past eight and we knew she got up early. It was mid-June and already warm, and I hadn't realised I was still in my pyjamas. I quickly went back to our apartment to get my dressing gown. There was no time to dress.

We rang again. Where was she? Why wasn't she answering? What was she doing?

I rattled the gate. It made a tremendous noise.

'Why did you do that?' Nicola said. 'You'll scare the old dear to death!'

The part of the villa our landlady lived in was some distance from the gate, so the rattle needed to be loud enough so she could hear it. Surely she would understand our anxiety - that's if she knew about our anxiety.

But she didn't.

'What if she's not in?' Nicola said.

'She's always in,' I said. 'She never goes out.'

As if to prove me right, she suddenly appeared from behind her bedroom *persiane* (shutters) on the top floor of her four story villa and shouted down to us.

Although Nicola's voice was raised, she spoke with a convincing impression of calm. 'Excuse us Signora,' she said. 'We have lost our kitten. Have you seen him?'

The landlady said she hadn't. She also said it was news to her that we had a kitten. She asked us if we had a photograph of him.

'No,' said Nicola, 'we didn't take one, because we never thought we were going to lose him!'

'That's a pity,' she said. 'Describe him to me in case I do see him.'

'He's gorgeous,' we said. 'He's lovely. He's beautiful. He's our baby.'

'I don't want to alarm you,' our landlady continued. 'But there are a lot of foxes in these parts, and they eat kittens like yours.'

I wasn't interested in talking at cross-purposes about our kitten's impending doom. I just wanted to get into our landlady's garden. But then she must have thought that was the end of the conversation, because without another word she closed the shutters.

'Doesn't she realise we want to look around her garden?' I said to Nicola. Then it dawned on me: of course she didn't, because we hadn't asked her. Nicola pressed the intercom button again as I rattled her gate once more.

We continued where we had left off, but this time I did the shouting. 'Excuse me Signora,' I said. 'We are sorry to disturb you again, but could you please open this gate so we can search your garden for our new kitten?'

Once again, with no sign of an acknowledgement, she closed the shutters.

Five long minutes later she arrived, fully dressed, at the gate, which she opened to let us in. She watched as we searched, bemused as we called out in English. We didn't really know what to call out, or for that matter, in what language, because we still hadn't decided on a name for him, and even if we had, he hadn't been with us long enough for him to recognise it. We made the universal sounds that cats seem to respond to, like whistling and finger clicking, plus other peculiar clicking noises; but there was no response.

However, when we began calling out in Italian, our landlady suddenly went from being uncertain to actively helping us. She changed her slippers for a pair of shoes and then took charge of the situation. She produced a bunch of keys and opened the gates of her estate, to allow us into parts of this eighteenth century former *convento* (nunnery) we hadn't known existed. I wasn't going to argue with her taking over the search if it meant we were going to be reunited with our kitten. She told Nicola to search the bushes at the end of her sizeable garden, while she took me by the hand down a flight of stairs that led to her *cantina* (the wine cellar). It was cold, as cold as a cantina is supposed to be. As I was still wearing my pyjamas, I noticed the cold all the more. She instructed me to lift empty wine barrels so she could look underneath them; but there was nothing. We looked inside dusty old crates and under tarpaulins, then we moved into her abandoned stable (which was full of crumbling antique furniture), but still there was no sign of him. After spending about ten minutes in there, she and I went to search in an old outhouse, but after only a couple of minutes, she decided he wasn't in there either. After that, she instructed me to go and help Nicola search the bushes. They were trimmed well, but dense and all but impossible for humans to penetrate - but perhaps not impossible for a kitten.

We considered that he might have gone through the bushes and back to a small hole near the waterfall where he was born, but to get there he would have had to climb a three-metre high solid stone wall that would have been daunting for even the fittest adult cat.

So, we decided to thank our landlady for allowing us on her property and we returned home, feeling sicker and even more perplexed than we did half an hour earlier. We then sat down, heads in hands, to consider what we were going to do next. 'That's gratitude for you,' I concluded. 'We take in a kitten, do our best for him - and does he care?'

But we knew animals do unimaginable things, so we looked around our apartment once more, although this time, we did it in a more methodical manner. We went through the drawers and the wardrobes for a third time. Even though we'd just been through the kitchen units, we went through them for the fourth time, but still found nothing. At around seven weeks old, Roger was about the size of a rat. I'd heard it said that if there were a hole the size of a fifty pence piece, a rat could get through it. I wondered if a cat could do the same, so I unscrewed the back of the cooker and parts of the fridge. It was surprising how many holes we discovered that were the size of a fifty pence piece. Alas he wasn't inside either appliance.

We hadn't given up hope, but we knew the chances of finding him were dwindling, so we went outside to the piazza and searched there, but that was also in vain. Over the next few hours, if we saw somebody we knew crossing the piazza we would call to them from our kitchen window to ask them if they'd seen our gorgeous black-and-white kitten, but they all shook their heads. We would also call out to people we didn't know, who likewise were unable to help, although in our desperation we may have sounded as if we were blaming them for not being observant enough.

We knew that people who find missing animals sometimes contact vets in the hope that they recognise the animal and know its owner, so Nicola phoned Sandro the vet to ask him if anybody had reported him found. Sandro, though, couldn't help.

Nicola decided to write a description of Roger on a post card and put it in the newsagent's window, and she wanted me to do an illustration of him from memory. I did one, but she said it wasn't like him at all. Trying to draw a portrait without the subject *in situ* isn't easy at the best of times. Doing one under duress is even more difficult; so she drew one instead. In my opinion hers was worse than mine, but it had to suffice.

The despair we felt about losing him went on for at least twenty-four hours, until we finally had to accept that we had lost him. We both told each other to think about something else if we could, because it was upsetting us too much. We'd also started to blame each other for losing him, wondering who had left the window open, and why.

Then, at 0.3am two and a half days after Roger had disappeared, we were both asleep when simultaneously we both reacted to a faint sound. They say a parent will always wake if their offspring needs them, and we were both sure we had heard our kitten's cry. When we didn't hear the noise again, we thought we must have imagined it. Stress can do that to the mind. After we had convinced each other that we were having the same nightmare, we must have gone back to sleep, but when we heard the noise a second time, we both leapt out of bed and started to pull the place apart once more, by now we were convinced that it was Roger and, thank God he was close by. But where was he?

My reaction was to open the now-closed window and look out, in case the cry had come from the landlady's garden, but it was too dark to see anything. Then there was another cry. This time we were not dreaming, nor imagining things.

We were now certain it had come from inside the small chest of drawers on Nicola's side of the bed. We opened the drawers one by one and there he was: our tiny and delicious boy, wedged between the bottom drawer and the back of the chest, in a space fractionally wider than the diameter of a ten-pence piece.

It was impossible, we kept saying as we carefully eased him out of his hiding place. Then we kissed him and cuddled him. Then we scolded him. Then we kissed each other, more out of exasperated relief than affection. Then we blamed each other yet again. This time for not dismantling the chest of drawers earlier, even though its contents had been emptied out numerous times. Behind the bottom drawer was almost literally the only place in the entire apartment we hadn't looked. In the meantime, he'd been without food and water for almost sixty hours. He'd probably been listening to our frantic efforts to find him, but for some unknown reason he hadn't declared his whereabouts. He had only given a few tiny meows, but they were enough to reunite us and release the distress. I cannot remember if we got any more sleep that night, but we didn't care; we were so happy. We thought he had failed to survive; but there he was, sitting on the palm of my hand, smiling at us.

The world appeared to be suddenly a lot brighter now we had found him. Despite having Lucy for some time, there was still a lot we had to learn about feline behaviour. From reading more textbooks on cat welfare, we discovered that after a major operation, a cat tends to go to ground to recover from the trauma. Sometimes this entails hiding. The poor little chap had not only been through a serious operation, this was the first time he had ever been handled by humans and he was also being kept indoors instead of living in a hole next to the waterfall with his mother. He must have been really traumatised.

The books also advised us that to help familiarise himself with his new surroundings we should keep him in the house for at least twelve days. We should close all the windows, so he couldn't venture further, either to escape or to explore (why hadn't we read that before?). We followed that advice, gave him lots of attention and made sure he had the best cat food that money could buy. After the twelve days had passed, we allowed him to go out, but made sure he was not out of our sight. Each time he returned he was brushed, stroked, cuddled, kissed, fed chicken and told how beautiful he was so many times he must have thought we had gone mad.

It was now time to give him a name. I hesitate when it comes to choosing names, because there are so many to consider, but Nicola is never slow in coming forward. She gave me about fifteen seconds to come up with a name, because if I didn't have one in mind, she certainly did. I then made the mistake of shrugging my shoulders, so she jumped right in and - to my horror - she came up with "Roger." I asked her why she'd made such an uninspired choice but then she told me her boss's name was Roger. He was a nice guy, she said, but he was wet. I got the point. Roger the kitten was wet when I first met him. But that was only one of the reasons. While Roger the kitten was under anaesthetic for his repair job, we got the vet to neuter him. Nicola said that by the time she'd finished with her boss, that's the way he'd end up too!

Roger grew into a handsome cat, with a head that had the profile of a lion. His mood was constant; proud, but never arrogant, a perfectly balanced persona. He loved me as much as I loved him, which was a massive amount. Five long cuddles a day was the average we shared and he would remind me if we hadn't had them. Roger had style; he was turning out to be a gentleman cat that wore his black-and-white dress suit perfectly. His fur was of the finest quality; smooth and as shiny as silk, cool to the touch and it swayed in the mildest breeze. All that was missing that would have complimented his handsome appearance and his smart disposition was a bow tie on his white chest. In artificial light his eyes twinkled like black pearls. He was similar in looks to the cat in the Felix cat food advert, except he was much prettier; so much so that once I considered contacting Felix to tell them that our Roger was the one they should be using. He also had long black eyelashes. One day whilst I was admiring him I noticed them; they set his face off a treat. When I told Nicola, she came running to have a look. I believe she was envious. Later in life I noticed that not all breeds of cat have eyelashes. Not a lot of people know that.

Roger would be considerate towards the other cats that we would gradually to take in. An example of this took place every evening, when I would call the others in so we could all settle down for the night. If they were being a bit stubborn, Roger would help me round them up, as if he were a sheepdog. I hadn't trained him to do this. I put it down to his (admittedly short) time as a feral cat, which I think made him well aware that the evening is the most dangerous part of the day for a cat, or any animal for that matter, because it is the time their predators come out to hunt.

Rounding them up for the night and closing the door cost nothing. Failing to be vigilant leads to unnecessary vet's bills, or even the loss of a pet. The countryside around Lake Como has its quota of foxes, wild hogs and stray dogs; any one of them can make a mess of a domestic cat. Then there were our human neighbours to watch out for, because there were the odd one or two who would sometimes garrotte an unsuspecting cat with the intention of eating it. And they were not at all concerned if it happened to be someone's pet.

As soon as I sat down in a chair, Roger would jump on my lap, because it was his opportunity to have a cuddle and a chat. He had got me where he wanted me and he didn't like it if I tried to get up. If I were thinking of reasons why I shouldn't be sitting down with him, he would know immediately. If I were going through a soothing motion just to appease him, he would know. He could tell the difference between a proper soothe and a one that was a ruse to lure him into a false sense of security. He could sense if there was real meaning in my fingertips or not. If I had things to do other than painting, I had to stay on my feet and make sure I didn't make eye contact with him, because if I didn't, he'd want me. He was patient up to a point, but when he decided I had been working for too long he would look at me, as if to ask why I was doing things when I should be sitting down, giving him my undivided attention.

Roger worried about my welfare as much as I worried about his. He was a worrier by nature and when he became the alpha cat among our expanding feline family, he took his responsibilities to heart. Although this was a self-appointed role, he was an excellent boss and he would keep them in check with a firm but gentle paw. He ruled in a calm way. He didn't need to demonstrate his position with outward signs of authority, because he had an air of authority that made the others respect him. None of us disputed his position or tried to usurp him, but I think it was only me that ruffled his dignity. He would often tell me off if I wasn't doing what he thought I should be doing. If that didn't work, he'd put on his disconsolate look.

Roger embodied peace and calm. Other cats arrived and, through misfortune rather than any lack of care on our part disappeared before their time, yet Roger survived to be an old man. I believe what kept him going was his love for me and mine for him. Towards the end, he became a little rheumatic.

The newer members of our family were more aggressive by nature and they could have taken his alpha mantle away, but they never challenged him. He was first to the food bowl and none of them would move to feed until he gave them the nod. Even if he wasn't in sight when the food was put down, the others would wait for him to arrive and to finish eating before their scramble for food began.

Roger was alert to every sound. He was enthusiastic about some of them, such the rattling of a box of cat biscuits, which would cause his mouth to water in anticipation of something appetising. Others he detested. He hated anything that fizzed, particularly aerosol sprays and ring pull cans, because they are similar to the hiss of an unfriendly cat. He wasn't keen on anything that crackled. Plastic bags being crumpled alarmed him, as they do with many cats. He would sit in his armchair deciphering noises that issued from the kitchen and decide if they were worth moving for. Ears pricked, he'd recognise footsteps and who they belong to - or whose car it was leaving or returning to the piazza.

Besides being obsessed by chicken, Roger was addicted to being brushed with a stiff bristle hairbrush. Brushing was good for his coat because it brought his natural oils to the surface, which made him shine like a polished limousine. When I brushed him, he would contort himself into all sorts of positions to get the maximum effect. He liked to be scratched too, particularly under his neck, possibly as much as he liked brushing. This made him dribble. If Nicola and I were sitting with him he would ask us to both scratch him as hard as we possibly could; so hard one might think it would hurt - yet he never once pleaded for respite. I'm sure he would only have called a halt to it if our fingers had barbed-wire tips.

Most days, I would leave the apartment at approximately the same time to go down a couple of dozen outside steps to work in my studio on the ground floor. Roger would always be right behind me. He loved being in the studio because he knew there was a chance I might be sitting down to paint, and that meant it was an opportunity for him to lay on my lap. Sometimes I'd ask him for his opinion about what I was working on, but he never showed any interest in art.. On the floor near to my work table I had put a three-sided cardboard box and placed a thick cushion in it. After a cuddle, Roger would make himself comfortable in it for the rest of the day. The box was intentionally open at the front so we could see one another and repeatedly kiss each other, cat fashion with slow, blinking eyes. When the daylight went and it was time to close up, he'd follow me back upstairs so we could continue to be near each other.

If I had to go out and Nicola wasn't around, Roger's smile would disappear and I could see sadness in eyes. Before leaving, I would put my shoes on at the very last second and try not to rattle the car keys in the hope that he wouldn't notice I was on my way out. But I was only kidding myself. He knew I was about to leave because he'd already read my mind. If Nicola and I had to go somewhere together, we had to sneak out of the apartment. We felt awful about leaving him because we knew he'd be upset. If we didn't manage to close the front door quickly enough, he'd follow us down Via Recchi, making the saddest noise he could muster. Even if we were only walking to the village to get some shopping, he would sound as if he believed we were deserting him forever. We never dared turn round to acknowledge him, because it was too emotional for us to take. His territory extended to a hundred-metre radius beyond the apartment and when he got to the end of it he would stop and wouldn't go any further. Nevertheless he would continue complaining as loudly as he could until we were out of sight. Then he would return to the house to await our return.

When we returned, the first thing I would do was look for our Roger, and we would greet each other with a "ciao", and a hug. A cat's meow sounds like "ciao", which is the familiar greeting Italians use when they meet a friend or family member. After the greeting, he would commandeer my lap for a few minutes while I apologised for abandoning him. He had a way about him that always made me feel I had to apologise, and make it up to him with lots of kisses and his favourite goodies.

When I went out in the car, and if he managed to squeeze out of the front door before I could shut it, he would make it as difficult as he possibly could for me to leave. He would race me to the car and then he would lie in front or behind one of the wheels, refusing to budge. Blowing the car horn repeatedly had no effect, and neither did firing up the engine. Bouncing up and down in the driving seat in an attempt to imitate car movement never fooled him and trying to get him out from under the car was like playing tag on all fours, because he would move from one wheel to the other. If I still couldn't grab him and Nicola was at home, I'd have to ask her to help. Eventually, with the aid of a broom we'd win. He would sooner get himself killed than see me go. If I was on my own and it wasn't an absolute necessity for me to go out, I wouldn't go. It was easier than scrambling about trying to catch him.

If I had managed to go out in the car he would know when I came back. Nicola said that as soon as he heard the car approaching the piazza, long before it came into sight he would leave his chair and come running to meet me. How he knew that this commonplace Fiat was mine and not one of dozens of others in the village was uncanny. I would greet him with hugs and kisses and as I carried him back to the apartment I would feel the anxiety he'd been harbouring while I'd been away leave his body. I was home. He was relieved and so was I.

Roger was a kindred spirit. There was only one 'Rog' in this world. I'm certain he was both telepathic and psychic: for example, if he had been out of sight for what I regarded as too long and it was enough to make me worried about his safety, all I had to do was concentrate on his image. If in my mind's eye I held a picture of him for a few seconds, he would turn up a few minutes later, often with an enquiring look to see why I wanted him. My wanting to see him for no reason other than my having concern at his absence must have bemused him.

It was a deep love Roger and I shared when he was alive. Five cuddles a day for eighteen years adds up to more than thirty thousand cuddles and that is what I reckoned we shared. Our cuddles were also an opportunity for me to whisper sweet nothings in his ear. The ones he cared for the most were: 'who's a pretty boy?' Followed by: 'pretty pussycat boy.' But his undoubted favourite was: 'Rog' is the best, but don't tell the others.' For harmony's sake and to stem feelings of envy in our other cats, I have to spread my affections fairly. Nicola is the eldest of four sisters and she recalls the unremitting rivalry between them when they were young, when they tried to get their parents to tell them which was their favourite daughter. If she heard me telling Roger he was my favourite she would tell me I must not have favourites, because it would make the others jealous.

Roger was my permanent shadow and my best friend. His concern was that every day passed as harmoniously as possible. With him around as my guardian angel, they usually did. Except for one day. We were in the apartment when Nicola heard a huge squeal. It was Roger, and he was hurt. Nicola responded first because she was beside the window, and she could see him. 'Quick!' she said, running out of the apartment. He needs rescuing!

I looked out of the same window, to see him hanging upside down from the top of our landlady's wrought iron gate, which was over two metres high. I ran to help Nicola untangle his left paw, which was twisted round, almost full circle. We knew immediately what had happened, which was something we had seen him do on several occasions. He would explore the landlady's garden and on his way back home he'd jump onto the top of the gate, gain his balance and slide down the other side. This time, though he had slipped and ended up hanging upside down with his paw trapped in a part of the ironwork. There was absolutely no need for him to jump over her gate, because he could have come back the way he entered her garden - through a hole in the wall further down the Via Recchi. But cats have their routines, which are logical to them, even if they make no sense to us. Now he was in distress and so were we. As Nicola supported his weight, I reached up and freed his foot. The skin wasn't broken, but we feared he could be lame for the rest of his life. I took him immediately to Sandro's surgery, where he was X-rayed. There were no breakages, but he had badly twisted his ligaments. He arrived home a couple of hours later with his foot heavily bandaged, and he stomped around for a few weeks until he regained his strength. Although the accident left him with a distorted foot, it wasn't that noticeable and it hadn't left him lame.

The average age of a domestic cat is reckoned to be between twelve and fifteen years, though a cat can live longer - as much as twenty years. It depends on its genetic background, the care, nutrition, exercise and regular veterinary visits. A cat's life cycle does not follow the equivalent in human years. The first year of a cat's life equates to fifteen human years, and the second year takes them up to an equivalent of twenty-four in human years. From that, add four human years for each successive year of a cat's life. In general, a feral cat doesn't live anywhere near as long as an indoor cat. Two to three years is usually the maximum, because their life can be threatened by starvation, traffic accidents, fighting with other cats, hypothermia, poisoning (accidental or intentional), disease and predation.

When the time came for Roger to go, I was in hospital with a broken vertebra. I'd been gardening and had fallen flat on my back onto a concrete path from a height of two metres. A few weeks before that had happened, Roger had started to suffer from a bloated stomach. He'd had diarrhoea for some months, and it had started to become progressively worse. He was then eighteen years of age, which is the equivalent of eighty-eight in human years. Nicola said I should prepare myself for the worst, because she didn't think he would be with us for much longer.

I didn't want to know about that.

When the moment came it had been up to Nicola to make the decision, because I was absent. I returned home after three days and nights, wearing a steel back brace and the first person I wanted to see, apart from Nicola, was my beloved Roger. Strangely he wasn't around. Nicola then had to tell me that she'd had to summon Sandro the vet to come and put him down, because he had started to suffer.

My Roger was, as they say where I come from, "the business". He was the cream on top of the milk. He was the quintessential conductor of the orchestra. He was an example of sophistication; born with what we humans endeavour to cultivate. He had it all, including exemplary manners. When we talked he would sit so proud he made me want to squeeze him. He spent half his life sitting next to my paint-box or my computer keyboard so he could be next to me. I can still see his shape to this day. Unfortunately there's a massive gap there now he isn't around to fill it. He left me alone and very tearful.

Roger was an orphan and he was adopted. He didn't have a pedigree; he was a common moggie - an expression he would have found as offensive to take as I do. It makes a cat sound like a piece of filth stuck to a shoe. A cat is far more majestic than that; each one deserves to be highly rated.

Roger was regal as well as outstandingly good-looking. His coat was more akin to finely spun silk than fur, and he would wash it until it gleamed. He was magnificent, and what's more, he was nice with it. He was a smoothie in the best sense.

What saddened me most - and believe me, I was sad almost to the point of despair - was that when his time came to leave us, I wasn't there to say goodbye. Eighteen years is but a smidgeon in time; but for Roger it was his entire lifetime. To comfort myself, I kept thinking (and I still do) that perhaps it was just as well I wasn't there when Sandro arrived to take him away, because I wouldn't have been of any help. I would have been too distraught. I have never asked Sandro how many times he's had to bear the anguish his clients must suffer when he's called upon to put an animal down. I guess somebody has to do it. I know it's a supreme act of kindness, but I don't know how they can.

Roger brought companionship, happiness and cheer into our life. He was - and always will be - my principal cat, and I miss him so much. I had an affinity with him that will never be replicated. He died on April 16, 2012 at ten-fifteen in the morning. As I write this, that was five years ago and yet I still think of him every day. It has taken me three attempts at writing his story and whilst I've been telling it, I've found out I am still grieving for him. I wonder if he thinks of me.

Thankfully, Roger survived to old age, which these days seems to be an achievement for an animal in a world that is getting progressively more crowded. He was the first feral cat we had adopted and during his life he shared his domain with all the cats we have had since we came to Italy. In the eighteen years he was around, he witnessed nineteen other cats come and go. At this time, five of the nineteen are still alive and mercifully in good health..

Roger

6 Antonio, Raffaello and Alfredo

Antonio was the second cat we adopted. He was white with a black hood and a few black patches on his rear. His ears had black points and they turned backwards at the tips, like those of a lynx. His eyes were a fascinating green colour and they were more oval than those of most cats, which gave him something of an oriental look. Ants, as we came to call him, belonged to the third generation of feral cats we had witnessed roaming the piazza. I would always keep a close eye out for any new kittens or cats to see if they were in good condition, and it was as I was looking out that I saw him for the first time. In the company of his mother, he walked right past my studio door, on what must have been his first ever walk outside his den.

I knew where Ants had been born. I had seen his mother coming and going through a hole in a thick wall further down Via Recchi from the waterfall and I guessed she'd made a den inside it. She was an ordinary brown tabby, very similar to Roger's mother, but she disappeared off the scene soon after her litter started to roam, as indeed Roger's mother had done after she had presented him to me. Ants' mother had been hanging around the piazza for some months and left three other kittens, all males from the same litter.

There were two tabbies: one a dark brown and black mackerel pattern, and the other a lighter brown mackerel with a cream chest. The third was black and white, similar to Roger. However, rather than stay around the piazza he tried his luck higher up the steps towards the back of village. We occasionally saw him outside the house of Bepe, the local builder and his wife, Nadia. I believe Nadia fed him regularly, but she wouldn't let him in the house.

We adopted Ants the day I found him asleep in Roger's box in my studio. Roger was also asleep in it. Sometimes I would leave the door open to enable tourists to view my artwork at their leisure and he must have wandered in. He had also finished off the rest of Roger's biscuits. When I closed the studio that evening he followed Roger and me up the stairs to our apartment as if he had been doing it all his short life. After he had had another good feed, the three of us settled down to await Nicola's return from work and for her opinion regarding a further adoption. She didn't protest, so his adoption was confirmed.

Of Ants' brothers, the dark brown and black mackerel tabby was particularly pushy. If he saw a glimmer of light around our front door, he would push it open and make his way to Roger's food bowl. One day, when he'd filled his face, he went into the lounge to join Roger for a snooze on the divan. When we saw him there, he looked at us so pleadingly that we let him stay. I'm glad we did. We named him Raffaello. His arrival took our number up to three.

You may wonder how we chose Antonio and Raffaello for our two newer arrivals names. On the opposite side of the piazza to our apartment was a dentist's surgery, and the two men who ran it, Rafaello and Antonio would join us for morning coffee and a chat. When we first met them, they were dental technicians who were studying to become dentists. They needed guinea pigs to train on and this was handy for us, because in Italy, dental costs are frighteningly high. Nicola and I volunteered for them and over a period of two years we had approximately €6,000 worth of work done for free.

So, in the way of a thank you for their efforts, Nicola decided to name our new kittens Antonio and Raffaello, shortened to Ants and Lele. Antonio the dentist was a devoted supporter of the famous Torino-based soccer club Juventus, whose players wear shirts with black-and-white stripes, so he was happy to be associated with Ants.

Raffaello was also a Juvé fan and he would have liked to have his name linked to the black and white kitten, but he was content to settle for having tabby Lele named after him.

When Ants moved in, he adopted Roger as his mentor. He thought Roger was his best mate and would follow him around all day. He would sleep next to him for hours at a time, but I don't think Roger was as enamoured with Ants as Ants was with him. But they seemed to get on well enough, because I don't recall hearing a cross word between them. Just occasionally Roger had to remind him that he had been first on the scene and that, being six months older, he demanded respect. Hierarchy in the cat world has to be maintained, and some stringent management controls can come into play if it's forgotten.

Ants also took on the role of Roger's minder. If Roger was outside and trouble arose, one of his duties as Number One Cat was to face it head on. If it arrived in the form of a rogue cat or a dog and he was having difficulties making them understand why they weren't welcome, Ants, who had grown into a big cat would stand shoulder to shoulder with 'Rog' and flex his muscles, look the trespasser straight in the eye and growl until the invader was repelled. Yes, Ants could growl. When he was unhappy with something, he could register a note that always surprised us as well as the intruder. Lions roar; Ants growled.

Ants was considerate and well mannered. He would come home immediately he was called. He always kept his white coat immaculately clean and he had a really sweet nature. He seemed to behave himself beyond expectation. We had seen him suffer during the first winter of his life, when he lived rough and was always hungry and I'm sure it was because of this that he was eternally grateful to us for adopting him. A couple of days after Ants became an official resident, I took him to Sandro the vet to be castrated and to have a general check-up. He was thin, and like all ferals was suffering from worms. If he hadn't been de-wormed that's how he would have remained, the parasites in his gut becoming even more prolific. This had been one of the reasons he was always hungry, because the worms had been digesting most of whatever food he could scrounge. With the right medication he was soon rid of them, but what was more concerning to us was that he had a persistent respiratory problem. Sandro said it would probably disappear with proper feeding and sleeping indoors and after twelve months, it did. Ants' ordeal from his time as a *randagio* (a stray) was finally over. We kept him warm and well fed from then on, and it wasn't long before we all fell in love.

As we had done with as many of the males as we could catch, we had another of Ants and Lele's brothers castrated. We called him Alfredo. He was the lighter brown tabby with the cream chest, and we offered a home to him. Although he came to eat for a while, he refused to stay with us. Like the black-and-white cat Nadia fed, he seemed to prefer the feral way of life. It was his choice. Our door was always open for him. He continued to pop in from time to time to fill his stomach and when he did he would always acknowledge his brothers, but he never wanted to join in their lifestyle. Later, we would see him when we were out shopping in the village and he looked the worse for wear, with bitten ears, sores on the back of his neck and what seemed to be a damaged eye. We'd offered help, but if he turned us down, what more could we do?

Where Ants and Lele remained strong, healthy and clean; Alfredo became old before his time, and he looked uncared for, as happens with feral cats. Where contented, domesticated cats wash constantly, ferals seem to give up the ghost.

When the weather turned colder the flow of pregnancies abated for a while and with that, everything seemed to calm down; but come the springtime we took a head count of the feral cats in the main square. We were down to thirteen from twenty, but why was this? We had taken in Roger, Ants and Lele and we knew the whereabouts of Alfredo and the black-and-white one that Nadia fed, but some of the ones we had taken to Sandro to be neutered seemed to have disappeared. We wanted to know where they had gone. We hoped they had not been eaten, but anticipated that some of them probably had - as well as dying from disease, infection and predation. We never found out exactly why each one disappeared and as you might expect, we never would.

Alfredo

7 Samantha, Ferragosta, Kubanski, Arturo And Pam

Traditions run deep in Italy, so when a couple of foreigners such as Nicola and me happened along and tried to change decades, if not centuries of embedded culture by telling certain people not to eat cats, their task would be akin to rolling a one-ton boulder up the side of a mountain. And when it came to our neighbour, Alberto, the task was all the harder, if not impossible. Alberto was more than fat. He was obese. Even these days, where obesity in Europe is approaching epidemic proportions, it is rare amongst Italians because most are extremely conscious of their appearance. The term *bella figura* (beautiful figure) is an important one to Italians, but Alberto couldn't care less what he looked like.

He was a retired plumber and boilermaker, and his girth must have measured two metres. His diet consisted of the worst in mountain food, in respect of the amount of fat and carbohydrates it contained. The mountains around Lake Como are famous for polenta, cheeses, Po valley rice, bread and *pizzoccheri*, a ribbon pasta made with buckwheat. It is all wholesome stuff, but you'd be wise to keep the portions small, otherwise you would end up with a waistline like Alberto. Game of all varieties is also in plentiful supply, as is the freshwater fish from the lake and Alberto would welcome all he could get. He didn't actually shoot, trap or fish the game, but he knew people that did. He would then order it from them in copious amounts, and devour it in equal measure. With someone who has an appetite like that, it is hard not to suspect them of making a meal of a feral cat, and enjoying every morsel of it.

We never did have any evidence of him doing so, but we always had our suspicions, especially when one of our cats, a particularly vulnerable one was lost for good.

From having Roger, Ants and Lele we attempted to reset the gender balance by acquiring three females. The elevated viewpoint of our kitchen window enabled us to see the ferals clearly as they roamed the piazza. Some of them were true street-wise survivors, but some were not and they needed help if they were going to live. Besides feeding them from bowls we placed near our front door, we helped by throwing food to them. For the ones who were slow off the mark, we would throw the scraps as far as we could so they would have a fighting chance of getting some. That is, except for a pretty, all-white fluffy one that was always too slow out of the starting blocks. Even if our aim was true and a scrap or two landed at her feet, the others would snap it up before she had realised what it was, so we had to make a decision about her. Because our apartment was so small we couldn't take every stray, so we had to be selective and decided to take the ones we believed couldn't fend for themselves.

It can be extremely traumatic for a kitten that hasn't had human contact before to be suddenly and unexpectedly taken away from what they are used to. A kitten doesn't know the difference between somebody who wants to give it a safe home and somebody that wants to kill it, but this one looked so vulnerable and not cut out for the rough and tumble of feral life. She seemed only too willing to be nabbed.

On the very the day we took her into our family my daughter, Samantha happened to telephone us to enquire about us and also about the cats. When I told her that Nicola and I were discussing what we would call our latest addition, she said, 'why don't you call her after me?'

According to a glossy book we have about different types of cats, Samantha the cat could have been a Turkish Angora. She was around four months old and she didn't have much vitality and she didn't seem to be that interested in going out for exercise. She preferred to hang around the place, look pretty - which indeed she was - and sleep a lot. In fact, she stayed indoors for a whole year before she decided to venture outside. Her lack of mobility meant she became overweight, and the fluffiness and whiteness of her beautiful coat made her look even bigger than she actually was.

A little while after we had taken in Samantha, we took in her sister. The day we took her in was Ferragosto, Italy's August public holiday, so we feminised the name of the holiday to make it Ferragosta and that's what we named our new kitten. She was another of the more vulnerable ones that we took in, and she took the number of black-and-white cats we had up to four; Lele, the dark brown-and-black tabby being the odd one out. Although she was from the same litter as Samantha, Ferragosta's markings were almost identical to Ants'. The only way we could tell them apart was that she was slightly smaller, and her black hood wasn't as symmetrical as his. In character though, she was a lot different. Her movement was slower, and she seemed old before her time. Although she was still a kitten when we adopted her, I don't remember her playing much. This is not uncommon amongst strays because playing is associated with having fun; and I can imagine there aren't many occasions to have fun if you are trying to survive in the wild.

We called her Ferra for short, and she was useless as a cat. I don't mean this in a derogatory way, but like Samantha she couldn't look after or defend herself. Although they had both been born in a feral state, I for one had supposed they would be street-wise enough to handle themselves if or when the occasion arose. But they weren't. As soon as they became indoor cats they both put their complete trust in me, especially Ferra. When she was in our apartment, like her sister Samantha she had no real desire to go out, although she did like to sit in a particular sunny spot in our landlady's garden if the spirit moved her. When the rest went out to play she would stay in, preferring to look sweet and have nothing to do with other cats. She had to be persuaded to do what cats are expected to do. It was as if we had taken in an old person who needed to be cajoled into activity. I recall two harrowing occasions when she was crossing the piazza on her way home from sun bathing in our landlady's garden. Two dogs that had been let off their leads approached her and she froze, bristling with sheer terror. If I hadn't arrived quickly to rescue her, I dread to think what would have happened. Most cats in situations like these will put up stiff resistance or run away, but I believe Ferra would have been killed.

Samantha did venture out sometimes, and even when she wasn't always in view she was always within earshot. When I called her in, she would come in within moments. Rather unexpectedly, one morning I was called to meet a client in Milan. Because I estimated I would be away for at least six hours, I would have to make sure all our cats were safely inside the house, with enough food and clean litter trays provided for the rest of the day before I left. Samantha was out of sight when I was about to leave, but when I whistled and called her name she did not respond. Rather than be late for my meeting, I had to leave without getting her in. The first thing I did when I returned was to call her, but she still didn't turn up. This was very strange, so I asked some of the neighbours if they had seen her. Signora Rosa, the eyes and ears of the piazza said that soon after I had gone out, Samantha had returned to the house, but as the door to the apartment was closed, she sat on the doorstep for a couple of hours. When Signora Rosa looked again, Samantha wasn't to be seen.

Alarm bells started to ring in my head. When Nicola arrived home from work we searched the surrounding area, but there was no sign of her. Next morning we still could not find her, and a week later there was still no sign.

Without proof it was impossible to accuse anybody of kidnap and as it was winter, which was the time of year when cats are most likely to taken and eaten and she was easy pickings, we were fairly sure she'd ended up on somebody's plate. We had no evidence to show this was Alberto's plate, but as I said, we had our suspicions.

The sadness that fell upon us again affected everything we did for the next few days. We just had to try and get on with life and hope the pain would lessen. But our pain was slow to fade, as it always would turn out to be when something tragic happened to one of our cats. From then on, we fitted all our cats with red collars in the hope that anyone who had a fancy for a cat dinner might be dissuaded from nabbing them. At least they would know it had a proper home, if nothing else. Nicola did the rounds yet again, informing the neighbours about the latest victim and advising them not to mess with our cats. However, the business of trying to persuade the diehards not to touch our cats was not yet over. Every time we thought we were getting through to them, something else would happen that made us realise we were taking two steps forward and one step back.

A few weeks later, to fill the gap Samantha had left, we took in another of the feral cats that we had already had neutered when she began to hang around our door. She was tortoiseshell and grey with some white bits and she was sweet natured, lively and cuddly. We named her Kubanski, after a Czechoslovakian work colleague of Nicola's. She was only too grateful to be allowed to stay, but a few months later, when Roger and I did the late evening round up she didn't come home. This was unusual and I was distraught. For several hours I searched for her, going well beyond a one hundred-metre radius of the piazza.

The next day Nicola put the word out that Kubanski was missing, and we were hoping she hadn't been eaten. The advice from our neighbours was that it was unlikely that she would have been eaten, because it was summer and cats only get eaten in the winter. This did ease our distress a little, but it wasn't going to bring her home.

We heard nothing for two weeks, then Marco, one of the local council workers arrived in my studio. I'd known Marco for some time. He lived only 200 metres from us in Via Durini, next to the blacksmith's workshop. Marco is a kind man and he tried his best to tell me the news I feared as considerately as he could, but there was no mistake when he placed a red collar next to my drawing board. He had discovered a cat down a ravine near the waterfall. For a second, I thought he meant she was trapped - therefore there was a chance she could be rescued - but he told me she'd been drowned. What had happened and why? I made further enquiries; a young girl said she thought she saw an old man, who lived in the house besides the stone footbridge push our cat off the wall into the ravine. She said she knew he had done this in the past to other cats. Even though he was eighty years old, I was ready to pull him out of his house and push him down the same ravine, but Nicola stopped me, saying there was no proof he had done it and that we could not take the word of a young girl who only thinks she saw what she saw. Still to this day I think there was proof that this person had murdered one of our cats, and I am sure that Nicola kept the whole truth away from me for my own and the old man's safety.

Word was clearly getting around about our activities; but either it was the wrong kind of word, or it was being conveniently misinterpreted. 'If you ever have a problem with a cat,' people were saying, 'take it along to Piazza Recchi, where two soft-in-the-head *Inglese* live. They will take care of your problem for you, free of charge.'

Soon after midnight one night we heard a muffled noise outside the front door, then the sound of footsteps along the stone stairway, fading into the distance. A few minutes later, we heard a faint mewing sound and it was not one we recognised. When we opened our front door, we saw that somebody had dumped a shoebox on our doorstep. When we looked inside, we saw a very young kitten. The next morning, after we'd give this gorgeous little creature several good feeds and a brushing, Nicola set off for the village in a determined mood, verging on anger with the box containing the kitten under her arm. Her intention was to root out the perpetrators, then give them a stiff lesson in how to take care of their animals. She was successful in locating them. She saw a group of young girls playing in the village centre and asked them if they recognised the kitten. One of them did. It was hers! It transpired the girl's cat had recently had a litter of three and her mother had told her to put the kittens outside people's doors in the hope that they would take them in. Ours happened to be one of those doors. Nicola made the girl take this particular kitten back to her home. What happened to it after that, we simply do not know, but at least we made it known to that family that we were not a dumping ground for any and all stray kittens.

It would take longer for our message to spread further, or at least for it to be taken seriously, because few nights after the kitten in the shoebox incident, somebody else dumped a runt kitten in the piazza. This time we were not able to trace the owner, but according to Signora Rosa they drove up the road in a maroon car when it was dark and dropped something out of the door. She suggested I take the kitten to Marco the council worker. One of his jobs was to dispose of any animals in a poor state of health that he found in the local area, and this baby was definitely not long for this world.

Nicola's determination to curb pregnancies seemed to have worked, because after two years' devoted work, there were no more litters born near to where we lived. But we found that the cats we took to the vet to be neutered never forgot the experience. And who can blame them? Being cruel to be kind isn't how they see it and it would make them extremely wary of the person who had transported them there. More often than not, that person would be me.

Like the loss of Samantha, the death of Kubanski made another hole in our lives. To fill that one we took in another feral kitten that had been struggling to find a meal. He was a white medium-long hair, with beige splash markings on a dark chocolate face and ears and we named him Arturo. There was a distinct similarity between his markings and those of Albury, the Himalayan rabbit we had kept in Godalming.

When some Italian tourists from Rimini visited my studio to buy a painting and when they saw Arturo and as we spoke about him, it became clear they were passionate cat lovers. I then told them how we had been trying to control the local feral cat situation, and how many we had rescued. They told us they would be only too willing to take Arturo, if I were willing to let him go. I must say I was a bit taken back by their suggestion, but perhaps it meant we could adopt another of the disadvantaged ferals; because there were still plenty of them in need of a home. I said that when Nicola returned home from work that evening, I would ask her if she was willing to let him go. I told the couple that if they would return the following day, we would give them our decision. After a lot of soul-searching, we decided to let him go to Rimini.

A year later, they walked into my studio with Arturo on a cat lead. They said that they took him with them wherever they went and they wanted to show him to me now he was fully-grown.

He was in excellent health, and it was wonderful to see him again.

A few days after we had let Arturo go to Rimini we took in an all-black cat with stunning, bright green eyes. We tried to adopt her because she had become pregnant far too early, and we actually witnessed her aborting under a laurel bush outside our landlady's front gate. It was a disturbing sight. I am a bit squeamish in a situation like this, but Nicola isn't and she helped her. The poor cat was in distress because her litter of four were not formed properly. They were at a late stage - quite large, and very much alive - and she didn't understand why they didn't react to her licking the way they should. It was as upsetting for us as it must have been for her to have given birth prematurely. Nicola took her litter away and tried to help her as best she could to forget her distress and by spending a lot of time with her, and offering her milk and tinned meat. Later that same week, we whisked her off to Sandro to be sterilised. At less than eight months old, he said, she was not physically mature enough to give birth properly. He also informed us that cats in general reach sexual maturity when they are eighty per cent fully grown, which means that in the case of feral cats, they usually reach sexual maturity earlier than indoor cats. However, for a successful birth, they shouldn't breed until they are at least eighteen months old. I believe she never forgot Nicola's assistance in her moment of need, because she and Nicola seemed to bond with each other from that time on.

Everything had to stop when this new cat required food and if it didn't, she would moan the place down. So, Nicola named her Pam, after one of our neighbours who also moaned a lot. Sadly Pam stayed indoors for only a month because, like Ants' brother Alfredo she preferred the outdoor way of life. However, she did stay close by for many years and would eat her evening meal with us.

Despite the fact that she ate regularly and heartily, she remained small and even when she was fully mature she remained a sleek, quick-moving miniature of a cat. She was so small, passers-by called her a *micia* (a kitten). She lived in a state of nervous anxiety, behaving as if she was in a rush all the time. At feeding time, she would dart up the stairs to the kitchen and insist on being fed without delay. There was never any 'please' or 'thank you.' But we didn't care. It was good to see her surviving.

Pam was a real beauty, with a silky, shiny coat and we were pleased with her, except for the fact that she resented being picked up. She would never allow it. I maintain that feral cats should be introduced to domesticity as early as possible for reasons like this; because if they are more than a few months old when they are adopted, they find it difficult to adapt to indoor life. Being stroked - and certainly being picked up - can be extremely torturous for them. We persisted, in the hope that she would get used to being handled, but she never did. On the few occasions we did manage to get close to her, we saw that her claws and whiskers were black, whereas on most cats they are transparent. Even her nose, the inside of her ears and the pads on the bottom of her feet were black, when commonly they are pink.

Although she preferred to live outside, Pam remained close to us in her own way. Almost every night, unless the weather was poor, she would wait for Nicola to arrive off the ferry and escort her the two hundred metres up the rise to our apartment. I could hear her talking to Nicola all the way to the front door, and of course I could hear Nicola responding. Nicola would then produce a plate of meat that Pam would woof down in a matter of seconds, and then be on her way. We believe she lived in an old disused wooden shed on an allotment, because I'd seen her climbing in and out of it through a hole, and she occasionally smelt of the old sacks that can often be found in such places.

It seems to be a fact of life that when it comes to owning pets, they are likely to die before their owners. Living with them will be to share fun and joy. In Italy the human population is an ageing one and if a pet owner dies before their pet it can be left to fend for itself. They say a pet is for life but whose life do they mean?

When we lived in Moltrasio there was a dear little grey and white cat that lived on the opposite side of the piazza who kept herself to herself. Unfortunately, her elderly owner passed away unexpectedly and when the *comune* (the local council) came to collect her body they locked the house up leaving her cat outside.

Roger was familiar with Signora Elena's cat and he used to visit her garden regularly to flirt with her, under the shade of a magnificent magnolia tree. For him to get into her garden it was necessary to climb a three metre high vertical wall. We called her his *girl friend* but of course it was a platonic friendship because he had been neutered. Nevertheless, his instinct must have been strong because from distance we had seen him more than once attempting to have recreational sex with her.

We had never actually met Signora Elena's cat but after she died it became necessary for me to enter her garden. The constant bleating of the cat to get into the closed up house was causing us and indeed Roger distress. Therefore, to save her from starvation it was time to rescue her and to do it I needed a set of ladders and a cat basket. A few minutes later we had another mouth to feed.

The one hesitancy we'd had about bringing a stranger into the house was would the others accept her because if they didn't then we would have to find her an alternate home. Fortunately all was calm, and as they touched noses we got the impression that they all knew her, which was comforting news.

However, there were problems ahead. She looked unsettled and within minutes of us taking her in, she decided to hide herself amongst the geranium plants on the window sill. Either that or she kept running to the front door to get out. Nicola's patience is exemplary when it comes to dealing with animals and she kept trying to content her by putting fresh tinned meat out but she would only lick the gravy sauce. She seemed to be of the small variety of cat and surprisingly thin and we wondered why? We didn't know her age but her coat felt dry and so did her nose and so we became concerned about her health. I lifted her on the kitchen table to examine her and soon found she had two bad teeth that were obviously causing her pain when she chewed. A couple of hours later I presented her to Sandro to have them removed. There was a further problem in store because in his estimation she was an old cat and when he squeezed her abdomen he said she had swollen kidneys and they were probably failing. He was concerned she might not survive the anaesthetic he was about to administer so he could pull her teeth, which was unfortunately what happened. After I took her back home to recover she never woke up.

Signor Tommaso was a retired, friendly neighbour of ours who had been a close friend of Signora Elena. He said he would bury her cat for us in his garden to save us having to pay Sandro to have her cremated. I had got to know Signor Tommaso well because he would visit my studio when he went shopping in the village. I had great admiration for him because he had been a partisan resistance fighter against both the Italian Fascists and the occupying Nazi forces in WWII. Although he didn't tell me many stories about the things he was involved in, a friend of his told me a lot more and it turned out that Signor Tommaso was a real life hero.

Nicola volunteered to prepare a shroud for the poor cat with no name and early next morning I took her in my arms to be buried.

Signor Tommaso's garden was only a hundred metres from our apartment and as I left the house Roger followed me. His girlfriend had passed away and he was well aware of it. More sadness was to come. When I arrived in Signor Tommaso's lengthy and well maintained garden he had already prepared a deep grave and lined it with straw. I let him lay the cat in the grave then surprisingly and very movingly he mentioned the cat's name in a short prayer. He then said "era giusto che il gatto dovrebbe essere reunite con la Signora Elena perchè lei amava molto Giulietta." (It was only fitting that Giulietta should be reunited with Signora Elena because she loved her very much).

Signor Tommaso didn't want me to give him a hand fill in the grave, so I left with Roger in my arms and as I did I thought it ironic that Signora Elena had died four days before Giulietta, yet her cat had been buried first. Signora Elena's funeral was to be held three hours later in the village church of San Martino.

When I returned to the kitchen where Nicola was looking as outwardly solemn as I was feeling. I said how upsetting the scene had been. "It seemed that Signor Tommaso was conveying his close affection towards Signora Elena through a respectful burial of her cat". I also said. "Perhaps it's as well that pets die before their owners because if they are without what they are used to, then it is all too sad to cope with."

For the next eight years, everything went fine. Nicola continued working in Milan and I was still receiving commissions to paint murals in the homes of the wealthy as well as selling watercolours and oil paintings of the lake from my art studio to the tourists who visited the village. Then, we were suddenly shaken out of our comfort zone by a series of significant events. The first one happened on the morning of September 11 2001, when an Al Qaeda faction destroyed the World Trade Centre in New York City.

A few days later, Osama bin Laden, Al Qaeda's leader issued the prophetic words: 'The world will never be the same place again.' He was right. That atrocity didn't do my business, or anybody else's any good, as tourists fled Italy on the first available plane home.

Almost five months after that, on January 1 2002 - a second blow hit us. It was the day the Euro was launched and it affected everybody in mainland Europe. It finished off any hope that the slump in the tourist trade caused by the 9/11 atrocities was a temporary one, as practically overnight the price of a holiday rose by twenty-five per cent, in line with the rise in the cost of living in the Euro zone. That spring, when the holiday season was supposed to be starting, the few foreign visitors who did visit my studio all remarked on how expensive they found Italy was compared to when the lire had been the currency.

The third reason that threatened our wellbeing was much closer to home. It happened three months after the advent of the Euro, on the evening of the eighth anniversary of our living in the apartment. A hand-delivered letter dropped onto the doormat, informing us that the rent on our flat would be increased by twenty-five per cent with immediate effect. As if this wasn't bad enough, a month later another letter arrived, demanding a separate rent rise of thirty per cent for my art studio. My immediate reaction was to confront our landlady over these considerable increases, but after further consideration, we decided to direct our energies into moving house. But, on asking around, it appeared that rents were being hiked up all over the local area.

Thanks to the Euro, property prices were escalating beyond reason, so rather than waste time squabbling over the rent of our flat, or waste even more time hunting for somewhere cheaper, buying a place of our own became our most immediate goal before we were priced out of that market too.

Unfortunately, we were in for another shock. After viewing only three properties for sale, we discovered we had already been priced out of Moltrasio, which had grown to become the twelfth wealthiest community in the whole of Italy. For such a small village to hold its own with the big cities was some accolade, but we could not hang around to appreciate it before it became the eleventh or even the tenth wealthiest.

Up until the moment our rents were increased we had not seriously considered buying a property, but after we had made the decision to buy, we knew that unless we won the national lottery we would have to look further afield. Seven years previously we had sold our Elizabethan cottage in Godalming, but we had been hesitant about entering the housing market in Italy because offshore investment rates had been satisfactory. But now, with a drop in interest rates and uncertainty within the global economy, people had returned to buying bricks and mortar as a secure investment. Suddenly we were being left behind; and we found ourselves trying to compete against an influx of highly-paid Italian and international present and past soccer stars, wealthy industrialists, business tycoons, politicians, oligarchs, property developers and celebrities - with the likes of entrepreneur Richard Branson and Hollywood film star George Clooney snapping up highly-desirable lakeside properties.

For over a year we felt cornered, with little hope on the horizon that we would be able to claw our way out of the feeling of melancholy into which our situation had landed us. Then, from out of the blue a minor miracle happened. A smart, detached, four-bedroom property appeared on an estate agent's website. It was a three-floor villa, built into the mountainside, just forty metres from the lake shore. It had terraced gardens, wide balconies, a garage and a stunning, spectacular, uninterrupted, twenty-eight kilometre view from north to south over looking the lake.

And, especially for our cats there was an expansive wood to the side of the villa we knew they would appreciate. This was a property we could really get excited about, especially as it was one we could actually afford. All this and it was only ten kilometres further up the lake from Moltrasio, in the lively and unspoilt village of Argegno. Five months of bureaucratic paper shuffling later, we were the proud owners of the villa.

Ants, Ferra and Roger

8 A New Home, Some Newcomers and a Lethal Intruder

After fourteen years of renting it felt good to be homeowners again. We looked forward to settling into our new home, but we had to be mindful of the fact that cats do not deal well with change. Even subtle changes in their environment can lead to stress, so moving house calls for care and the minimum amount of disruption. I went to our new residence the day before we moved in to prepare the place for them. I took some of their blankets and cushions with me and placed them, unwashed, in four of the separate chairs that the previous owners had left behind. I also took most of their favourite toys and one of the litter trays, along with their food and water bowls, so that when they arrived, there would be smells and objects with which they were familiar.

Before leaving Moltrasio, we told them where they were going and why they were going. More importantly, we told them that they would be loved and cared for just as they had always been, so they had nothing to worry about. We also told them that they would have much more living space, a large garden to play in and woodland beyond that. We also said there would be plenty of special cat treats to eat when we had moved in.

As soon as Roger, Ants, Lele, Ferra and Pam had inspected and approved the interior of their new home, they wanted to explore the garden. As all the books recommended, we intended to keep them inside for twelve days and nights to allow them to become accustomed to their new home. We knew this would be difficult to achieve, and it was. As we expected, Pam was unhappy about being locked up.

She moaned and complained continuously and she clawed the back door to tell us she wanted to be let out. We had hoped she would take to her new and much larger surroundings and within the extra space she would find a part of the place for herself, but she just wasn't a house cat by nature and it seemed unfair to keep her locked in. We had considered leaving her behind so as to avoid the distress we were causing her, but in the end we took her with us because we were concerned about her getting enough food. But after what can only be described as a cursory exploration of her new home, we realised we may have done the wrong thing by keeping her in, so we let her out.

Trying to keep the rest of them in and occupied with their favourite toys as well as some new ones also wasn't working, so forty-eight hours later we had to let them out as well. It had to be done at some stage, so we opened the back door, then watched them tentatively crawl into the garden a few centimetres at a time, their bellies almost touching the ground, as any cat will do when faced with a new environment. As they went, we assured them it was okay to proceed; as long as they didn't stay out for too long and we prayed they wouldn't disappear forever. Their noses worked overtime as they sniffed the ground and drystone walls, searching for recent scents. They were completely absorbed by this whole new world we had presented to them. Ants, the fearless one was the pathfinder, with the rest, including Roger following cautiously behind. As they crossed the lawn they looked left and right. Then they looked up and they liked what they saw. Within seconds, they had detected, as we had anticipated they would, the trail that led to the woods. Moments later, they were on their way up the mountain and soon they were out of sight. As with any animal, it is impossible for a cat to control its instincts. We knew there was nothing we could do from then on.

We put our trust in fate, and hoped that when they were hungry they would return. Within an hour, thank goodness they all did, seemingly lighter in mind and united in the opinion that we had chosen a grand spot for them. We greeted them with kisses and cuddles and the best quality cat treats.

We hoped that Pam would also return, but sadly she never did. She had well and truly packed her bags. But twelve months later, as Nicola was walking home one evening from the ferry terminal in Argegno, Pam appeared out of somebody's garden to greet her and escorted her along the pathway leading to our home, just like she used to do every night of the week when we lived in Moltrasio. Nicola said she could hardly believe it. Nicola instantly recognised her all-black coat and that familiar moaning voice. For weeks after, Nicola called her name outside the same garden every morning on her way to catch the boat, and every evening on her way back home, but alas, we neither saw nor heard Pam again.

Although Argegno is only ten kilometres north of Moltrasio, it is more countrified. Moltrasio sprawls and we had to walk for a good half an hour to reach open country. By contrast, in Argegno the countryside begins right outside the door and it would give our cats endless opportunities for adventure. Our villa is 280 metres (600 feet) above sea level and tall palm trees enjoy the sub-tropical microclimate. The mountains that surround the lake rise to over 900 metres (3,000 feet) and vegetation is more or less the same as it is in most Central European countries, Wildlife is abundant, and I soon got used to getting up in the middle of the night to chase away the wild boar, roe deer or feral goats that wanted to devour my flowers and vegetables. They were, and still are persistent in their attempts to rid me of the results of my hard work, as are an ample population of butterflies. These might sound less harmful, and you might say I should encourage them and there are some unusual and pretty varieties, but when their caterpillars hatch, they can quickly trash rose bushes and geraniums.

There also seems to be an endless supply of lizards, voles, scorpions, slow worms, field mice, rats and grass snakes. We also see the occasional adder and our cats have a wonderful time hunting them all. They will spend hours peering into holes and cracks in drystone walls, waiting for the opportunity to pounce. Like all cats, they will bring their trophies home for us to admire. Cats have a natural siege mentality when they hunt and they will sit outside a hole for hours, waiting and listening for movement. They organise themselves in pairs or as a pack, taking turns to keep watch. That inevitably means their prey doesn't stand a chance when it eventually makes the fatal mistake of poking its head out of its hole. Our cat books say that within a year, a cat will wipe out all wildlife smaller than itself within a hundred-metre radius of its home. I'm not sure this is true, because in the case of our lot, their years of hunting hasn't effectively reduced the number of unwelcome presents they bring us. Having said that, what amuses me is that when they are hunting they have the patience of Job, but when it comes to being fed by us, they are highly impatient and demand instant attention.

We had been living in Argegno for two years when we started to get visits from a cat we had never seen before. It had very similar black-and-white markings to Roger's and we wondered whose it was. We never encouraged it because it had a hostile attitude, especially when it came face to face with one of our cats. Having a stranger on its home territory is a humiliating experience for a cat, especially if the stranger is forceful and persistently tries to enter their home to steal their food. After several confrontations with it, our cats would look most indignant. Desperate and always hungry, ferals have no qualms about stealing any uneaten food. They behave like thieves and can leave you feeling just as violated.

A short while after this stranger began his sorties,

Ferragosta began to look thin. We thought it was because it was summer, when cats don't need to build up or maintain fat reserves. Even though she was eating regularly she continued to lose weight, so I decided to take her to see Sandro. He remembered the poor condition our cats had been in when they were feral. He would often compliment Nicola and me on how healthy they had become and what a good job we were doing. This made me feel proud, but on this occasion I was embarrassed. Sandro gave Ferragosta a thorough examination, including an X-ray of her intestines, but it revealed nothing. He gave her a vitamin injection which he said might help her, but after another week there was no change, so I took her back for another appointment. More tests revealed nothing and as he seemed baffled as to what was wrong with her, I suggested testing her for the Feline Immunodeficiency Virus, the feline equivalent of HIV. He and his assistant thought this a rather extraordinary request, because they said it was very unlikely to strike in this area. Nonetheless they took a litmus test, which within a few seconds proved positive. A cortisone injection helped pick her up for a few days, which made me hopeful she would recover, but I surfed the Internet for more information about the virus and discovered there was no chance of her surviving for more than a few weeks.

How had she contacted it? Sandro thought she could have been born with it and if so, it was most probably inherent in the rest of our cats. They all came from the same area and some from the same litter. But Ferragosta was now ten years old and had always been healthy, so why had there not been any sign of it before? Sandro said it was the first case of FIV he had come across in his area for years and he was concerned that it might be endemic.

Another week on, Ferragosta began to suffer. She was sleeping far more than usual and when she was awake, she was wobbly on her legs. From being a chubby five-and-a-half kilo cat, she became alarmingly thin. She was also becoming confused, which was excruciating for Nicola and me to watch, because she kept asking us what was wrong with her. Within four weeks of our noticing Ferra's dramatic weight loss, the moment had arrived for us to say goodbye. We phoned Sandro, and he decided he would come to our home on his motorbike to put her down immediately. Nicola is tougher than me when it comes to things like this. She had prepared a shroud for Ferra, but it was all too much for me to cope with. I was distraught. Poor little Ferra, she looked so weak. I shall never forget the bewildered expression in her eyes when she knew her time was up. Before I handed her over to Sandro we had a long, private hug in the kitchen where I told her I would see her soon. What really upset me and made me hide in the basement with a box of tissues until he had taken her away was her quiet, yet pleading little meow as I kissed her goodbye. I can still hear it seven years later. We hoped that the loss of Ferra was a one-off, but to make sure, we had the other three tested. Thankfully, the results proved negative.

A couple of weeks later, we had to pay another visit to Sandro's surgery for him to attend to a minor injury to one of our cats. There, we saw pinned on the waiting room notice board an advertisement showing a photograph of a wicker basket brimming with eight-week-old kittens that needed homes. We needed something to cheer us up after our recent bereavement, so we called the telephone number on the ad. It was answered by the sweet-natured Signora Luisa, a middle-aged lady who lived close to the Swiss border in the village of Maslianico, which was approximately fifteen kilometres from Argegno.

Sandro had told us she was well known in the area for taking in unwanted cats and advertising them in the various vets' waiting rooms and in free newspapers, in the hope that she could find homes for them.

When we arrived at her house, she had eight beautiful kittens from two litters running around her lounge. Only two of them were available, as she had already found homes for the other six. One was a white female shorthair with pink eyes, orange ears and an orange-and-white ringed tail. Her sister also had a ringed tail, but she was a grey tabby with a white chest, white legs, paws and face. It was just as well the others had already been spoken for, because they were so pleading and so gorgeous we would probably have taken them all.

To Signora Luisa's disgust, all the males had already been selected. She said this was normal, because the majority of Italians who have cats don't like having to pay to have them neutered. Thus they only want males because they don't want to be presented with an unwelcome litter. We already knew that to have a male castrated is considerably cheaper than having a female 'done', because it is neither invasive nor as time-consuming. During a half-hour chat, we told Signora Luisa a bit about our history and that of our cats, because before she allowed the two kittens to go she wanted to know if we were genuine cat people. She was especially curious to know how we had found her telephone number. To assure her we were genuine, we invited her to visit our house whenever she wanted, so she could see how two of the hundreds of unwanted cats she had rescued over the past thirty years were getting on. She said she appreciated the offer. We offered her money for the two kittens , but she refused it, telling us that if we take them it will be payment enough.

We were pleased to have found replacements for Pam who had left home and the recently deceased Ferragosta and we hoped that Roger, Ants and Lele would be as pleased as we were when they were introduced. During the drive back, I broached the subject of deciding on names for our new additions, before Nicola had time to think about it. I decided to call the all-white one with the orange ears and tail Anfield, after the name of the stadium where Liverpool Football Club play. I then gave Nicola the opportunity to name the grey-and-white tabby, because I also had a name in mind for her. Curiously, she also decided to call her after a soccer club. Not a big Premier League club like Liverpool, but a much smaller one, Crewe Alexandra. This was not because she had any association with the town of Crewe or with the club, but simply because she liked the sound of the name.

But, despite us having Ants, Lele and Roger tested, our troubles were not over. Exactly a month after we had lost Ferra, Ants began to look thin. We were devastated. Was it a coincidence, or was it because he was from the same mother as Ferragosta? We didn't need to go through the tests because it was obvious he had the virus, but we had had them tested anyway, on the very slim chance it wasn't FIV. More upset and tears followed when Sandro told us that the results of the tests were as anticipated. We took him back home for a week and spent a lot of time with him; but the day soon came when Sandro arrived on his motorbike to put him down. I disappeared into a downstairs room and said several prayers for his soul until it was all over.

Once again, Nicola provided a burial shroud. Sandro placed Ants in a specially made wooden box he had fixed to the back of his motorbike and took him to the animal crematorium.

It was a lonely few hours after Ants had gone. The interior of the house felt empty, especially the armchair he shared with his mate, Roger. The spot where he spent his last moments was still warm. This alone was enough to make me choke. Ants had become a real mate to me, as well as to Roger, and we loved him very much. It had all been so sudden. One day he was on form; the next day he started to go downhill and from then on he went fast. The saddest part was that he, like Ferra, couldn't understand what was happening to him. He was just eleven years old and always enthusiastic about life. He was strong, active and in his prime when he was struck. He'd had it tough when he was living in the piazza in Moltrasio as a kitten, but he had adapted to house life quicker than any cat I've known. It was almost instantaneous. He had loved being a house cat. He was still eating up until the day before he went, but when he couldn't manage to jump into his armchair, something that had been so effortless only a week earlier we knew it was time to summon Sandro. He had told us to call him as soon as he began to look weak and he would arrive within the hour. And he did. Thank goodness for Nicola, who is a realist when it comes to animals dying. I cannot handle it. I try to be strong; but I fail. She pulled me round by telling me that we had done our best and that there was nothing anybody could have done to save him. Dying is part of nature, so we must try and remember him when he was at his best. Nicola is not heartless. She still cries and crying seems to help her recover, but when I cry, it doesn't help me. When one of our cats dies, they take a part of me with them.

Two months later, Lele, Ants' full brother and Ferragosta's stepbrother began to look thin. We had him put down straight away.

I felt confident that Roger had not picked up the virus, because he had a different mother and he had been tested. Then it dawned on me that they weren't born with FIV. The three who had died had had vicious confrontations with the big black-and-white feral that was terrorising the neighbourhood. I knew this for certain because I had intervened during the attacks. I was now becoming convinced that it was an FIV carrier and the ones we had lost had all been bitten by it. It was then I decided that if it returned, it had to be caught then removed, but how to catch it was the question, because it was very elusive.

A month later, Anfield started to look frail. She had been attacked several times by the black-and-white predator and had stopped going out because she was terrified of it. I was furious and now was wholly convinced it was this intruder that was doing the damage, because Anfield was most definitely from a different litter from the three that had passed away. She was from Maslianico, ten kilometres from Moltrasio, where our lost three were born, and she was only a year old, whereas the others had been ten and eleven. Unfortunately I had become convinced too late to save Anfield and when we lost her it became imperative that I caught the menace before it infected Roger and Crewe Alexandra, the only two cats we had left. The problem was, though, how to avoid the danger. Locking cats in the house for twenty-four hours a day would be nigh on impossible, because they had always been able to come and go as they pleased. This period would be akin to guerrilla warfare, because the menace would strike without warning and disappear - and we were losing the war.

Crewe Alexandra

9 The End of the Menace and Some More Additions

Despite my determination to catch and dispose of the intruder, I had some questions that needed answering. A vet will not put an animal down without a good reason, if I rocked up at Sandro's surgery with the intruder, saying I wanted what looked like a healthy animal put down I would not be made welcome. Besides possibly having to answer other awkward questions, I also knew I would have to pay for the tests he would need to carry out and then pay even more money to have it put down and cremated. All this, for an animal I had started to loathe would be far too complicated, when all I wanted was to get it well away from our property. When it disappeared for several weeks I began to hope it had moved on and our problem was solved, but it turned out to be a false hope, because it returned and started once more to menace not only our cats but also those of our close neighbour and friend, Rico. He lives three hundred metres higher up the mountain and during a conversation Nicola was having with him in his village bar he told her that he'd also had to have one of his two cats put down, because the same aggressor (or so it seemed after he had described it) had been jumping through an open window during the night and had subjected the cat to a vicious attack. For me, this was even more confirmation that the menace was infected and had to be eliminated.

Placing poisoned food outside came to mind, but in doing that, we might accidentally kill one of our own. I did consider hiring Gianfranco, one of the village council workers who had offered to sit in the garden with his gun, all night if necessary, to get it.

After a short deliberation I thought it best to forget the idea, because the cat was cunning beyond belief and for sure it would sense there was something amiss. There was also a risk that Gianfranco might mistakenly hit one of our cats. I told Gianfranco that I had tried to sneak up on the cat several times with the intention of grabbing it, but it would vanish before I got within twenty metres of it.

I was becoming obsessed with catching the menace. I'd never before wanted to see an animal dead, especially a cat, but I did with this one. European wild cats do exist in the Lombardian mountains and for a day or so I imagined that it might be a genuine wild cat doing the damage, especially in the way of aggression. But when I found some information about wild cats, I discovered they are pretty rare and they look like a very much larger version of the domestic black or brown mackerel tabby. In comparing this proactive aggressor to a real wild cat, I might be doing genuine wild cats an injustice.

In my opinion this mystery cat had originated from a feral litter some distance away and it had wandered into our area in its search for food. Nicola, Rico and I had asked residents all over the area if they knew who owned the cat, but nobody did. Another indication that it wasn't somebody's pet was that it was grubby, with matted fur. And when it raided, it consumed four times the amount of food that a properly fed domestic cat would eat. I still didn't know what sex it was, because I hadn't been able to get near enough to it to see. I didn't know its age either, but I estimated it was around three or four years old. Of course none of this made any difference, because it still had to be got rid of. If it had been a human being, it would have been incarcerated ages ago. It had to be caught, and I ran all kinds of plans for how to do it. But catching it would be a difficult job, because it was cunning, fierce and quick.

Then it made its first mistake. It happened at about two o'clock one summer morning when we were in bed.

Because it was hot I had left our bedroom window open to let in some cooler air. Something woke me up and I caught a glimpse of the intruding cat leaving our house via the open window. It may have sneaked in with the intention of eating our cats' food, which was on the kitchen floor. When I went into the kitchen, I saw that all three food bowls were completely empty. It was then I realised that if I were to stand any chance of catching it, I had to be as cunning as it was. The kitchen was over twenty metres from our bedroom window, so before we went to bed the next night I made sure the food bowls were full of fresh, tinned food, the smell of which he wouldn't be able to resist. Around two o'clock, he arrived for his free feast. He filled his belly and as he was making his way back to our bedroom window to leave, we met head on in the corridor. He was very surprised to meet me and I tried to grab him, (by now I was close enough to see it was a male), but after a brief skirmish he managed to get away. Although thwarted, I was not defeated, because he had given me another idea. The next night I put out a bowl of the most aromatic tinned food we had and I hid in wait for him, but he didn't turn up.

Three nights later he reappeared, this time earlier than usual, at around eleven-thirty. I had just gone to bed when, in the half-light I saw him jump through our bedroom window and head towards the kitchen. I lay still, giving him a few seconds to get stuck into the food. Then, as I left our bedroom to follow him I closed the window and then the bedroom door behind me as quietly as possible. Barefoot, I snuck along the corridor that led to the kitchen and snapped the kitchen light on. Of course he freaked when he realised he had been caught and he bolted past me to make his escape through the bedroom window. He couldn't have known of course that I had closed the bedroom door.

He started to panic, running around the rest of our open-plan apartment, looking for another way out, but I'd made sure there wasn't one. I then opened the door to our sunroom, which leads off the lounge. He thought I was letting him out, but as soon as he rushed in, he realised was trapped, because there were no other exits except the windows, which were closed. I left him there for a few minutes to simmer whilst I prepared to do battle. I knew from past experiences when dealing with ferals that they will always put up a fight and by the size of this one, I knew it would be a tough scrap. Although FIV is a different strain from HIV, I wasn't keen on being bitten, so before I tackled him I put on some protection. I changed my slippers for shoes, put on a pair of thick corduroy trousers over my pyjamas and then put on my heavy waterproof coat, a pair of goggles and my gardening gauntlets. I picked up a metal cat carrier I had at the ready and I entered the sunroom, shutting the door behind me. He was well and truly trapped and he knew it.

For those who have never encountered a trapped feral cat, I can say from experience their behaviour redefines "ferocious". If it means ripping their captor to bits to escape, they will try their darnedest to do just that. This one turned out to be twice as mean as any I had come into contact with before, possibly because he was bigger and stronger. He must have weighed seven kilos, where an average, generally malnourished feral weighs half that. The only furniture we have in our sunroom is a low, wicker coffee table and two basket chairs. In his vain attempt to escape, he jumped on them all several times and, impressively he jumped up the windows, almost touching the ceiling. He was not only trapped, but he was also furious at being trapped and he tore around the room, searching for an exit. Twice he tried to leap off the coffee table and gouge my eyes out with his claws. I'd read in books how cats, like cornered rats go for their attacker's eyes, which is why I was wearing goggles.

Like a boxer dodging a punch, I sidestepped and he flew past my shoulder. My tactic now was to chase the beast around the sunroom so as to drain his energy, and to lessen some of his ferocity. I made sure he had no chance to stop for a rest and after a few minutes it was noticeable that he was beginning to feel the pace. He was breathing heavily and he had started to slow. He realised he wasn't getting by anywhere tearing around a room that had no obvious escape route. He needed a change of tactics.

I had him trapped in a corner of the tiled floor and, as he was trying to figure out what to do next, I made my move, which was to get him into our metal cat carrier but how to do it successfully was the question because as I approached him he started spitting and snarling and trying to claw me. After three failed attempts to plonk the cat-carrier over him, I managed to force him in with my feet and legs. And it wasn't flab I was pressing against. It was solid muscle.

I snapped the door shut on the cage, finally trapping him. With energy renewed by rage he tried to batter his way out of the cage and to claw and bite me through the grilles. Fortunately, the grille bars are too narrowly spaced for a cat's paw to pass through, though this one was trying his best to get at me. I had to be very careful when I took up the cage handle, because he still had plenty of fight left in him and with real fury he aimed his claws, the size of small daggers at me.

Now I had him, it was a case of what to do with him. I hadn't thought much about that, because I was never sure I was going to catch him. There weren't any law enforcement officers around to take him away, so it was up to me to rid our lives of him. I must say after the brawl I was slightly giddy, a bit breathless and sort of nervous. I was certain I had done the right thing by catching him, but now the ordeal was over and we had both calmed down considerably he didn't look half as menacing as he had earlier.

To my surprise, I started to feel sorry for him and I began to have second thoughts about wanting him destroyed. I had set him up for death, but I didn't want to be the one responsible for doing the deed. Even though he had killed four of our cats and I detested him for it, when he looked at me with pleading eyes I knew I had a further dilemma. It wasn't his fault he was carrying a deadly virus and I almost found myself opening the cage door to let him go.

It was now midnight and with no vets available to administer the fatal injection I decided to transport him as far away as I possibly could. I took the cat carrier to the car and put it on the back seat and without having any particular direction in mind I drove in the direction of Como city. Then, after seven kilometres I decided to take another right where I knew there was a large area of open farm land…Then I let him go.

The oddity was that, throughout the journey he didn't make a sound. In the past, when I had transported ferals we had caught to the vet to be neutered, they were extremely vocal, especially when they sensed the movement of a car for the first time in their lives.

Back in bed, I felt relieved that the threat to our cats' lives was now over. I was pleased at how my plan had worked out and in the morning I told Nicola (who had been oblivious to the noise of the battle) about what had taken place. She seemed even more relieved than I was. But, three days later, lo and behold, the menace returned. I was in the garden near to the where the woods begin when I saw him, standing around thirty metres away looking at me. As soon as he realised I'd seen him he shot off, no doubt remembering our confrontation a few nights earlier.

All went quiet for two more weeks and I was beginning to believe that our exhaustive tussle might have scared him off for good. In a way, I was right. Rico gave me some encouraging news when I popped into his bar.

He said he was so fed up with the menace attacking his one remaining cat and stealing her food he had done exactly the same as I had done. He had trapped him, fought with him and when he'd got him he passed him on to his cousin who had a boat. His cousin then transported the creature across to the other side of the lake, where he let it go. We celebrated over a glass of vino, knowing that unless the menace was prepared to walk a hundred and fifty kilometres around the periphery of the Lake Como to target our cats specifically, we shouldn't ever see him again. Seven years on, we haven't yet done so.

Nevertheless I've never been able to relax completely, because I recall reading an on-line bulletin about an Australian couple that had moved two thousand miles to a new home. Three weeks later, their cat disappeared, but almost two years after, they received an email from the people who had bought their old house. An attachment to the email was a photograph of their missing cat, which had turned up at their old home. But I suspect, and Nicola agrees with me, that most probably Rico passed the cat over to his "cousin with the boat", so the feral could be drowned in the lake, but because Rico knows we love cats he probably softened the story to one of abduction in case he upset us.

Within a month of Anfield's passing, Nicola took a telephone call from Signora Luisa, asking us if we had space for two more kittens she had ready for adoption. With Pam having seemingly left us for good and four lost to FIV, we decided that now the menace was no longer around, and the remaining two found to be free of the virus it was safe to adopt again. And so we set off in the car with two cat transporters to take the kittens Signora Luisa was offering us. She was waiting for us outside her house when we arrived. It was good to see her again, because we have great respect for what she does.

On our first visit, we had seen eight of the little darlings on offer, running around her lounge and it had been a fantastic and memorable sight.

This time was different. The two she had up for adoption were inside a small birdcage on the sideboard in her dining room. They were from the same litter; smoky grey and white shorthairs that were so identical that even when Signora Luisa pointed out which one was the male and which one was the female, neither Nicola nor I could tell them apart. But the occasion was to prove memorable because of the horror story she told us. 'They are caged,' she said, 'because they always have been caged.'

The twins were only about five weeks old when Signora Luisa received them, which was nine days before our arrival. This is far too young for kittens to be separated from their mother. They had been left in the birdcage outside a filling station on the outskirts of Como and they were covered in their own excrement and urine. Signora Luisa had come by them because the person who found them knew she was well known as a cat rescuer and had delivered them to her in the hope that she would be able to find homes for them.

But the most alarming part was that when Signora Luisa opened the cage door to take them out so we could have a proper look at them, they hissed and spat at her. She put on a thick glove, but immediately she put her hand into the cage they attacked it and viciously. She persisted and managed to get hold of the male. She placed him on her dining table, but the poor creature was too distressed to allow us to touch him. She told us that the person who found them had managed to clean them as best she could and Signora Luisa herself had since managed to bathe them, despite them scratching her badly. The way they behaved she said, made her think they had always been in the birdcage and they attacked anyone who tried to handle them because they were terrified at the thought of having to leave it.

Signora Luisa told us that when they were brought to her, they were very undernourished and dehydrated, but after Sandro had given them vitamin injections and a general check over, and she had fed them high protein milk and wet food, thanks to her care, they were now healthy and clean.

She wanted a decision there and then as to whether or not we were prepared to take them, but I was unsure. When I tried to lift up the one on the table to see if we could handle him, he yowled loudly. It was an incredible racket for such tiny creature. Nicola was more upbeat than me and said she was sure that in time they would calm down. Signora Luisa agreed with her, so we decided to take them. To save them further distress, we didn't transfer them into our transporters but took them as they were, in the cage.

During the drive back to our house I became doubtful about our decision. I asked Nicola several times about what we were going to do with them if they didn't settle down, but she accused me of being needlessly pessimistic. When we arrived back home I placed the cage on our kitchen table and they appeared calm, but when they believed a hand was about to enter their cage, they went crazy. I had no idea how we were going to clean them or the cage, or how to feed them if they wouldn't allow us near them. I was also concerned that because of the terrible start they had had in life they might be permanently messed-up psychologically and that they would never settle. And if they didn't, what were we going to do with them? As always, Nicola's attitude was far more positive than mine. She told me that animals are not psychologically messed up. It's the people that treat them so badly that are psychologically messed up.

Wearing gardening gloves, Nicola managed to pull them out of the cage, one by one. She then put them and the cage on the kitchen floor, so as to allow them to go wherever they wanted in the house, but they immediately jumped back in the cage and huddled together like frightened children. I decided to build a much larger cage in the sunroom out of timber and chicken wire, just like I had for our rabbits to run around in back in Surrey. It was two metres square and a metre high, with an entrance door so we could walk into the cage when necessary to clean and feed them. In one corner of the larger cage we put food, water, fresh milk and a thick woollen blanket for them to sleep on and in the opposite corner we placed a fresh litter tray. With the two kittens still in it, we placed the birdcage in the centre of new cage. We left the door of the birdcage open, in the hope that they would eventually come out of it, yet still have a sense of security. Of course we kept a close eye on them for the rest of that day and evening and made the occasional visit during the night. The next morning they were still huddled together in the birdcage, apparently asleep, but the good news was the food had been eaten, which meant they must have left it at some point in the night. We were still finding it difficult to tell them apart, especially when they were huddled together. They looked so sweet, as if butter wouldn't melt in their mouths, but we had experienced just what they could be like when they were awake and under threat.

Before long, we actually saw them leave the birdcage to eat. They also drank plenty of the fresh milk, which would help strengthen their tiny bones. After that they had a long sleep on the blanket. The next day I was able to take the birdcage away, forcing them to get used to the larger cage. A day or so later I left the gate of the large cage open. Gradually they started to investigate the sunroom and slowly but surely they ventured into the kitchen. It all seemed to be working and within a week I was able to remove the larger cage, because they were now venturing all over the apartment. They were also using the litter tray as if they always had done so. Soon they started to sleep on the divan in the lounge and within another week they would let us handle them; gingerly at first and not for more than a few seconds, but there were definite signs of progress and thankfully they had stopped hissing, spitting, biting and lunging at us with their tiny, needle-like claws. A few days later, as we were watching TV they climbed on our laps and settled down for a cuddle. In all, four weeks after we had brought them to Argegno the improvement in their behaviour was remarkable.

Roger and Crewe Alexandra had of course realised they had guests within seconds of them arriving from Signora Luisa's house, especially when Nicola placed the birdcage on the kitchen floor to enable them to give its inhabitants a good sniff. We had watched Roger and Crewe's reaction, because we were as interested to find out what it would reveal about future relations between them. Certainly they were curious, if not a little apathetic. Whatever they thought, within half a minute they had retired to discuss the matter in another room.

I believe that when the kittens eventually met Roger and Crewe nose-to-nose outside the chicken wire barricade, it reassured them that they were in a cat-friendly zone. That helped settle them quicker than if they had been alone and it seemed they were eager to be adopted not so much by us but by Roger and Crewe; so much so they began, when they were allowed, to follow them around the house. Neither Roger nor Crewe were keen on being followed wherever they went and on occasions they would turn round and give their hanger-on a gentle but firm bop on the nose. Fortunately, on the whole they seemed to accept them, at least for the time being.

For us, once an animal is named it becomes an official member of a family and I'd had plenty of time to think about names for them. I would like to have enough cats so I can name them after the players in the Liverpool soccer team (for those who aren't familiar with soccer, that is eleven). Nicola of course had different ideas.

On this occasion she decided we would name one each, and hers wasn't going to be named after a Liverpool player, or any other soccer player for that matter. She liked the sound of Kalashnikov, the name of the famous Russian firearms designer. In time we reduced it to 'Kalash.'

I held firm to my original plan and named the male

kitten Stevie G after Steven Gerrard, the legendary Liverpool FC star.

Stevie G

10 Crewe Alexandra, Stevie G and Kalashnikov

Crewe Alexandra is not the prettiest cat we have, but she makes up for her average looks by being brainy. She and her sister Anfield, who is no longer with us were the two short hairs we got from Signora Luisa to replace Ferragosta and Pam. Crewe, as we call her is what a stranger would describe a typical tabby. She has a grey and black striped back, a matching ringed tail and a blonde belly. Her face, chest, legs and paws are white and her eyes are yellow, but she is more than just typical. Crewe is what I call a proper cat, because she is intelligent, rational, analytical, wise and composed. And if needs be, she can handle herself. She looks down on the others and they look up to her. Some of the cats we have had have been mercurial, even nervy, but not Crewe. She is valiant and resolute and she knows her own mind.

When Crewe was a kitten she loved to play the Silver Ball Game on the lounge floor. This consisted of me kicking a small, tightly rolled-up piece of aluminium cooking foil around the room and her chasing it. She played the game with great intensity and at an electrifying pace. Her reflexes were amazing, but her energy levels faded away after a few minutes. She also liked to play football with a ping-pong ball. This was essentially the same game, except we played it in the long corridor that separates our lounge from the kitchen and bathroom. Before we commenced, I closed all the doors so the ball didn't end up in another room. Crewe always chose the same end of the corridor to stand and we would pass the ball to each other with our feet. As in the game proper, the loser was the one who failed to stop it going past them the most often. There is nothing worse than playing a game with an animal or a human who hogs the ball, but cats in general are not selfish. Crewe was typical of that and her ability to pass the ball back and forth with uncanny accuracy was a skill to behold. Coaches in the soccer world must wish their players had such natural ability. Cats are also good goalkeepers because their reflexes are electrifying, therefore, they block or parry every shot with consummate ease. Consequently I always lost.

I learnt from experience that taking in a cat is a new opportunity to be in love. And I like being in love. I've found that when a cat falls in love it is forever. Once smitten, their love can be trusted and they remain faithful. Crewe is a one-person cat, and her "one person" is me. I call her 'daddy's darling' and she wishes we were the only two creatures on the planet. I discovered she wanted to be my only cat as she grew to maturity, because she became visibly mystified why I allowed the others to curry favour with me. She appeared to regard them as intruders. At first she would put them all in their place, but after tolerating life with them for about two years, she decided to move from our apartment to the cantina on the ground floor. From then on she would only frequent our apartment first thing in the morning and last thing at night to have some milk.

When Stevie G and Kalash, the brother and sister that had been locked in the birdcage were eight months old I took them to Sandro to have them sterilised. When I went to collect them he said that although it was exactly the right time to have them sterilised, the operations had been awkward to carry out because they were so small. Even when they were fully-grown they remained small, like Pam. Both extremely pretty and fortunately they soon forgot about their terrible start in life, because their behaviour became normal.

I wish I could have taken the person or persons who had abandoned them outside the petrol station to be sterilised. I think if I ever witnessed anybody being cruel to an animal, I don't think I could control myself from being cruel towards them. It hasn't happened yet because abusers are a cowardly lot and they do it out of sight. Penalties for animal abuse are far too lenient and there should be severe punishments handed out.

Stevie G and Kalash have bright pink noses that have the effect of lightening their faces. They were so identical it took Nicola and I months before we could tell which was which, even close up. When we got to know them better we discovered that the white mark on the bridge of Stevie G's nose was slightly off-centre, whereas his sisters was central and his nose turned up slightly at the end. Stevie G also has the most amazing, doleful and strikingly beautiful eyes, akin to those of a wolf. They have pale blue irises and even paler green outer rims but these are not so clear from distance.

We call Stevie G our part-time cat. Once cats have marked their territory they will generally remain within its boundaries, but not Stevie G. In the summer he will go AWOL and won't return for several days, even weeks. This wanderlust was most disconcerting to us until we came to expect it. On one occasion he was away for five weeks and we started to believe that was the end of him. We knew there were no aggressive cats close by, but what worried us greatly and still does is the presence of predators further afield, either on four legs or two. When he goes away, Nicola, in her usual level-headed way will tell me not to worry, because he will back when he's hungry. And up until now he has always come back, fortunately unscathed but not ravenous. I call these episodes his dirty weekends. I'm certain he has a woman somewhere in the neighbourhood, because when he finally does return he smells of perfume. We don't know who she might be, but she must live higher up the mountain, because that is the direction he comes from when he decides to return.

When he does remember where he lives and decides to

come home, we can hear him long before we can actually see him descending through the dense foliage on the mountainside. He calls to tell us he is on his way and for such a tiny creature he has an unmistakable, forceful meow. Once he has announced himself he will belt into the house at top speed, faster than any other cat I've ever seen. He will climb up me as if I am a stepladder and sit on my shoulder, like a parrot. Most of the time I will let him climb up, except when I'm wearing a decent sweater. Then I am reluctant to let him, because it will mean it will get covered in unsightly pluck marks. When he returns, we have a celebration. We are so happy to see him once again, having several times given up hope that we ever will. He probably thinks this is good and the cue to go away more often, because instead of being scolded he's hugged and fed special treats.

At the time of writing, this smoky grey and white, fluffy darling with his sweet pink turned up nose and wolf's eyes is eleven years old. Because he is still tiny, when visitors to the house see him they think he is still a kitten, but he is a perfectly proportioned adult. Because he is so cute our visitors want to touch him and if he's in the mood he will sometimes allow it, but if he isn't he will hide under the furniture until they get fed up trying. According to the books we have, cats find it difficult to digest human food, but Stevie G's digestive system must be contrary to the norm, because he doesn't seem to have any problems with much of it. Perhaps it's because he has Latin blood that he likes Sicilian salami, but his real favourite is *Spaghetti al carni-trita* (spaghetti with a mince meat ragu) lasagne and *spaghetti aglio olio peperoncino* (spaghetti in olive oil with garlic and chilli peppers) are runners-up. I'm with Stevie G on the spaghetti aglio olio peperoncino. It's a favourite of mine too and one of my specialities. When Stevie G eats spaghetti, he sucks it up quicker than I can and the race is on to beat him.

He is also partial to *caprino* (goat's cheese) and likes

Italian ice cream for dessert, but then who doesn't? It's the best ice cream in the world.

Stevie G is so sweet, but then I think all cats are sweet and I believe they know they are, which is why I find them so captivating. They know that all they have to do to catch someone's heart is to be sweet and most people melt and then they give them what they want. Every pose a cat strikes looks like it is from a picture book. They are gorgeous beings to have around the place, but then I am biased.

Nicola accuses me of encouraging him to have bad habits, because I will allow him to jump on the dining table to sample what we are eating. Nicola and I don't row about many things, but this is one of them. She will ask me what would happen if we have guests for dinner and he decided to jump on the table. I tell her that is very unlikely, because if we have guests he will make himself scarce. Nevertheless she will continue to maintain that feeding animals from the table is the worst thing you can do, because it teaches them to beg. Stevie G doesn't ask for much but I wish he wouldn't jump on the table. It gets me into such trouble.

Despite his cheating, Stevie G is always forgiven when he climbs onto my lap for a cuddle. And when he cuddles, he cuddles. He likes cuddles that last for hours, and they would if I didn't have other things to do. I also call him my meerkat, because he will sit on his hind legs with a straight back. His pointed face and poky little nose that turns up at the end make him look so cute I could squeeze him to death. When he's in my arms he loves to lay his head on my shoulder and press his face as close to mine as is physically possible, so I can give him a beard rub. The harder I rub my stubble into his neck the deeper and louder his purr will be and I can increase the volume if I whisper pleasantries in his ear.

There were two dramatic incidents that involved

Kalash and lizards. Being cold-blooded, lizards need to bask in the heat of the sun to warm their blood. Until they have warmed up, they are in a state of lethargy and when they are like this, cats will toy with them, pull their tails off and then kill them, but as a rule they will never eat them. When one of these incidents with Kalash happened it was the height of summer. I was working in the garden and she was helping me, when suddenly she began squealing like a stuck pig and running around the garden in a frenzy. Eventually I caught her and found that she had a lizard in her mouth. When it wants to kill a small animal, a cat will catch it by the neck to asphyxiate it. Somehow, the lizard had got into Kalash's mouth and bitten into her gum. Lizards have teeth like tiny needles and jaws like vices and this lizard was causing Kalash intense pain. I managed to get the lizard to let go, but that wasn't the end of the story. A month later she was under an aesthetic in Sandro's studio having a bad tooth removed from the gum that the Lizard had bitten into.

Kalash later developed a fever. Like any cat with a fever she went very quiet, sleeping too much and going off their food. We took her to see Sandro, who X-rayed her and found that she had swallowed a whole lizard. Once again she made a mistake and one that could have been deadly. She had caught this lizard by the head and it had crawled down her throat, ending up in a foetal position in her stomach and was very much dead. Sandro said that Kalash would also have been dead within a couple of days if he hadn't pumped her stomach when he did, because a decomposing lizard is highly toxic.

Like children, cats can be loving and affectionate, but they can also be cruel to each other. Roger, Ants and Ferra got on well and I cannot remember any hostilities between them. Perhaps we became lulled into believing their sociability was the norm in a clowder.

When we took in Kalash and Stevie G from Signora Luisa, their relationship with Roger and Crewe Alexandra went swimmingly for a couple of years. Then, most unexpectedly a problem arose that involved Kalash, which was never resolved. Kalash was a sweet darling and like her twin brother Stevie G was very pretty, but after two years of living together, Crewe decided she didn't like her anymore. From then on she gave her a torrid time, attacking her every time she saw her. To the casual onlooker a cat fight is nothing but a cat fight, but the cats that take part suffer emotionally for hours after it's over and Kalash suffered every time she saw Crewe. Crewe wasn't that keen on Stevie G either, but he was and still is capable of looking after himself, whereas Kalash was the defensive sort. She became terrified of Crewe and moved herself downstairs to my studio, never to return to live in our apartment.

I would feed her, clean her litter tray, fluff up her bedding and give her a cuddle. It might not sound like much work, but doing it twice a day for two years it became tedious. I also had to protect her as best I could from Crewe, because if she wandered into my studio, all hell would break loose. I felt deeply sorry for Kalash and her situation. With Nicola's help we tried everything we could to mend their relationship, but it actually exacerbated the problem. Kalash loved company and now she had become lonely and frightened, so when I worked in the studio I tried to give her as much individual attention as I could. I would sit her on my knee and talk to her, calling her by her favourite pet name, "kitten cat".

Kalash would occasionally leave the studio to take the mountain air, but if Crewe came across her, she would set upon her. If I heard them I would dash outside to break it up, but mostly these fights happened too far away for me to do anything. All I could do was scold Crewe after it was all over and try to reassure Kalash with cuddles and some special treats, but the bullying continued and we didn't know what to do to halt it.

We couldn't and still don't understand why some cats

get on with one another and some don't. I guess it's the same as with people; some get on with others, some don't. I think Kalash appreciated our trying to keep the peace and keep her apart, but it was no use. Crewe had resolutely decided that she was not prepared to accept her any longer and to aggravate the problem, when Kalash did venture out of the studio, Crewe would block the door so she couldn't get back in. Sometimes, Crewe would hide behind one of the pot plants on the veranda, waiting for Kalash to return, then suddenly spring on her with claws unsheathed. The poor little girl didn't stand a hope and one day she never came back. She had obviously had enough.

The reason why Crewe had been treating Kalash so badly came to light within a matter of days of her leaving. It was because Crewe wanted to take over the studio for herself. When she was certain she had got rid of Kalash for good she moved from the cantina on the ground floor to the first floor. When Crewe is in my studio she changes character. She is sweet and embracing. She will even sit on my knee, but she will never do that in our apartment. She has made my studio her den and she likes me to work there, because I am not only company for her but she likes to talk to me. But I cannot be company for her all the time. I have to go upstairs to do housework and spend time with Roger. and as I go I always invite her to follow, but unless it's her milk time she always declines. If it is she will sit next to the fridge to tell me she is ready. Words will rarely be exchanged. There's no need; she has me well trained. I used to ask her if my beauti-fluff was thirsty-wursty and would she like her milky-wilky, but Nicola put a stop to that. 'She doesn't like baby talk,' she said. 'She would much rather you talked to her properly.' I'm sure Nicola is right.

Whether my beauti-fluff will agree, I don't know.

11 La Brigata Rossa - Ulisse, Fernando and Francesco

I fancied adding a couple of ginger cats to our collection. Perhaps it was coincidence, but the next time Signora Luisa telephoned to ask if we could take more orphans, I asked her if she had any ginger cats. She said she did, so we made an appointment to go and see them. This was just before we had lost Kalash, so our intention was to acquire two, to make our total up to six, the same number we had when we lived in Moltrasio.

When Signora Luisa opened the door to her lounge, there were, as anticipated two tiny balls of ginger fluff, asleep on a green rug. When they moved in their sleep, I could see that they were the most beautiful creatures imaginable. Nicola and I melted on the spot, like gelato in the sun. Rather like a salesperson, Signora Luisa will try and persuade her visitors to take several of her wares, but on this occasion there was no need for her sales talk. She already had a captive market. It was love at first sight and what impressed us most was the brightness of their ginger fur. Gorgeous isn't a good enough adjective to describe them, but as there isn't another in the English language that fits the bill it will have to suffice.

Italians call ginger cats "red". A cat with darker markings may also be called a *gatto marmellata* - a marmalade cat, because the colouring is reminiscent of orange peel in a jar of marmalade. However, these two weren't the only ones Signora Luisa was hoping to off load. There was another kitten sharing the same rug. Rather than ginger, he was a sort of all over dusty beige, with a champagne-coloured shell on his back and champagne blotches on a beige face.

He didn't look related to the other two, but Signora Luisa assured us he was their brother and that she had taken all three because their owner intended having them put down if she didn't.

We told Signora Luisa we'd only brought two cat boxes, so we wouldn't be able to take him, she told us he couldn't be separated from his brothers, because he would be lost without them. Without consulting me, Nicola said, 'what the hell! In for two, in for three. Throw him in a transporter as well.'

On the way home we were both thrilled and excited at having acquired three handsome kittens. We hoped that Roger, Crewe, Stevie G and Kalash would be just as thrilled. As I drove, we decided on names. Nicola said she was fed up with soccer players, so we decided to call the two ginger ones after our two computer technician friends Ulisse and Fernando. Ulisse and Fernando were abbreviated to Uli (not to be confused with Uli the baby bird) and Nando. The champagne coloured brother we called Francesco, abbreviated to Franco. This was the name of our general practitioner friend, who, like our new kitten was tall.

Most cats we've had hate the rain because it restricts their outdoor activity. They will sit by the window staring in disbelief at the falling raindrops, as if their plans for the day have been thwarted. They will turn and look at me is if it's my fault for causing the inconvenience and I expect me to think of ingenious things to do to keep their minds occupied. But our two marmalades have of an entirely different outlook on rain. They don't mind getting wet, or even soaked. In fact, they relish it, but I don't know if this is particular to marmalades. They like the snow as well. For Nicola and me, having two wet cats leaving muddy paw prints over our marble floors and mud stains on our furniture can be inconvenient, so I give Nando and Uli a quick dry with a towel when they arrive home.

They don't appreciate this and they will try and slink away from it, but I persist.

Nando and Uli have grown up to be beautiful cats, particularly Uli. According to an American lady who rented our holiday apartment, he is show standard. Her reaction when she saw him was 'WOW! Where did you get *him*? We don't get cats as red as him in the States.' She told us that she'd been a cat breeder for many years and used to breed plenty of red tabbies but ones with such pronounced markings as Uli's are very rare. She said Uli was special, "a happy accident of birth."

So, not only did we find out how special Uli is, we also learned a new term - "red tabby". Some people are under the impression that ginger (or red) cats belong to a specific breed. They do not. They are simply a different shade of tabby. Females of this colour are very rare. The two primary colours in a red tabby's genes are black and red (genetic symbol "O").

All cats have 19 pairs of chromosomes including one pair of chromosomes that determines the sex of the animal and the colour. Typically, females of any species have two identical XX sex chromosomes and males have two distinct XY sex chromosomes. The Y making them male. The gene which makes a cat ginger (or red) is located in the female X chromosome and it will override all other colours. Since males only need to have the orange gene in one chromosome to become ginger, and females have to have it in two, ginger males outnumber females three to one. As most red tabbies - ginger cats, marmalade cats or whatever you want to call them are male. Uli is what is called a mackerel-pattern tabby, which is the most common type of marking. He has hooped stripes on his tail and legs and bull's-eye swirls on his abdomen. He also has the classic M-shaped marking on his forehead. Nando is also strikingly red and with the classic M-shaped forehead marking and he is covered in mackerel tabby markings, but they are not as pronounced as Uli's.

In my opinion as an artist, whoever it was who chose to call ginger cats "ginger" or "red" must have been colour blind. If I were to paint them, the colour I would select would be burnt orange. The skin of fresh ginger root is beige in colour and the flesh is a pale yellow. The colour of dried, ground ginger is more likely but to me it doesn't have the brilliance of a ginger cat's colouring. The only connection I can make to ginger is possibly because the root has a fiery flavour and this description could, I suppose be applied to their character, because burnt orange cats are certainly fiery in temperament. Some people refer to them as fiery redheads and the books say that ginger cats are naughty cats. I've found ours to be more boisterous than naughty and certainly more energetic, mischievous and fun-loving than a regular cat, so I can understand why they have been labelled naughty. In fact, I sometimes refer to our two as *Il Brigato Rosso* (The Red Brigade) after the notorious Italian terror group of the 1970's, because if they are in the mood they can be terrors. They certainly keep us occupied, but we wouldn't change them for the world. For sure, we will never be accused of being couch potatoes whilst the burnt orange ones are around.

Nando adores cuddles and when we have them it makes him salivate. I call him a "dribbly-drooler". It's a shame to have to turn him away, but if I don't I can end up soaking wet. If I lie down on the sofa and he sees me, he will want to join me. This is a moment he has been waiting for since the last time I laid on the sofa so he can jump up on me then start "padding" my chest and stomach. Experts are unsure as to why cats do this, but they say it is what they did when they were kittens to stimulate the flow of their mother's milk. I believe cats do it as a prelude to sleep. Nicola says he thinks I'm a duvet and he's pressing the lumps down. Whatever the reason is, he likes me to stroke him while he's padding me. This will make him dribble and drool even more. And he's the only cat I've known who will lie on his back encouraging us to stroke his belly. He must trust us implicitly, because all animals protect their underbelly. If that gets damaged, it can have fatal consequences. I will continue stroking him until he wants to move to the corner of the divan so he can suck on his favourite cushion. I don't know if he was taken away from his mother too early but I suspect he was because he still has the need to suck, and he relishes it most if he is being stroked at the same time. And he likes to talk. If he's been out, he makes a noise that sounds like "ciao" when he returns. He likes to sit on my knee to have a chat and as we do he will watch my mouth closely, trying to look into it. The source of where the sound comes from seems to fascinate him and he will try his best to respond with grunts, chunners and more "ciaos".

Uli is an obsessive finger licker. Every time he comes for a cuddle, prior to him having a sleep or immediately after it he has an insatiable need to lick my fingers for several minutes. It seems I have to be the first and the last thing he sees in the course of his day. He, like Nando regards me as his surrogate parent and he cannot do without me. Not one of my cats has needed to be with me for as long as I allow it in the way Uli does. Not even Roger. I believe it is because he is insecure. It can come to the point when I cannot do what needs to be done because of the attention he will insist upon me giving him, which usually means my lying down so he can sleep cradled against my neck. When he was tiny, I would take him to bed with me at night and cradle him in my neck. I could feel his heartbeat and his purr vibrating against my throat.

Uli and Nando are brothers in every sense. They wander around the house, the garden, the woods and the mountain together. They also sleep together; and after ten hours' sleep at home during the day, they will have their main meal as the evening arrives, before getting ready to go out.

At around eight o'clock they will come back in for

another feed. They will then spend the rest of the evening watching TV and having a cuddle and a nap with us on the divan. When we go to bed they will transfer themselves to our bed for a further sleep, before going out again at around three in the morning. They will return once more at dawn for breakfast, which will be followed by a well-earned sleep. Their twenty-four hour cycle is so consistent that if I wore a watch I could set it by them. I know all their habits and of course they know mine, because they formed them; once you've adopted a cat, your life will no longer be your own. Cats involve extra maintenance but the reward for their devotion is their unwavering love.

Uli's love for me is the real deal. This marmalade show-standard cat gets so excited with being in love that his tail puffs up. We call it his Basil Brush tail, after the 1970's TV fox puppet character. He has claimed the entirety of our apartment as his territory and he follows me everywhere within it. He isn't fond of anybody else, not even Nicola. We believe he regards her as a rival for my love and if he is in a jealous mood, he will bash her if she tries to come between us. If I sit down and give him love in exchange for his he will swamp me, firstly with kissing. Cats kiss with their eyes. They save eye contact for the ones they love and they do it with a slow blink. He will look into my eyes and blink. Then he'll purr a huge purr and swish his magnificent, fluffed-up tail. He will stand in the middle of a room and give this tail, with its cream tip a happy swish. It's a swish that should be accompanied by the crashing of cymbals or a fanfare. (If that were to happen, he would leap into the air in fright!) After he has swished his tail, he will lick both my ears and then of course lick my fingers until they start to become sore from the roughness of his tongue. The only time he will leave me alone is when he wants to sleep. Even then he will want to snuggle into my neck.

He doesn't seem to understand that now he weighs seven kilos I have to push him to one side before he suffocates me. Roger was deeply in love with me, but if love can be measured, Uli's is all encompassing.

Ulisse

After lunch, I usually have a short nap on the divan and if Uli is not already waiting there for me to join him, he will be anxious to come and join me. Moments of closeness with an animal are some of the best experiences I've ever had. They feel so rare and special. Life seems drawn out on occasions but when I am physically close to my cats I can't help thinking of how short it is. We don't have very long on this planet and cats have even less, so it often feels as if we are in a race to fit in as much living together as we can before our respective plugs are pulled.

Uli is fully-grown and although he is supposed to be mature he is, emotionally still a kitten. He is hopeless without me. He doesn't seem to be able to cope unless I do everything for him. His brother Nando, or "Nandy Pandy Pudding and Pie" as he prefers to be called is a lot worldlier than him and I believe he does his share of looking after his brother when they are outside, especially when they are in the unpredictable environment of the woods and the mountains. When Nando is alongside Uli, I feel relieved of my duties for a short while, safe in the knowledge he will take care of his brother. Then, as they depart Nando will turn round and give me his "not to worry" look.

Uli loves to play the Rubber Band Game. When I say, "play", a cat's play isn't how we humans consider play. We play our games with rules and laws and we don't try and kill our opponent. A cat's rules are entirely the opposite. Uli can smell a rubber band as soon I take it out of a drawer and he will want me to hold it so he can take the other end between his teeth and stretch it to its full extent. He will then let it go with a snap so it hits my fingers. I think he enjoys hearing the snap, or maybe it's my pain. He is also attracted to the smell of pencils. If I am drawing or sharpening one he will snatch it out of my hand and chew until he's destroyed it.

Nando's favourite game is the String Pulling Game: we play it with a piece of tired-looking fur, tied on the end of a three-metre length of string. It's supposed to be a mouse. He knows it's not real but he still kills it with as much rancour he can muster. Over the years we've bought a variety of cat toys from pet shops, to keep all of them entertained. A battery-powered hamster on wheels that ran round and round in ever expanding circles kept them busy for a day or two and an elaborate furry tarantula that bounced up and down on a spring provided a brief spell of fun, until they ripped it apart. We've bought a laser that throws a beam of light up walls that they can chase, but they soon worked out where the beam was coming from. Now they sit in front of the laser to block it. We bought several catnip mice, rubber balls with bells inside and a radio controlled toy rat, all of which entertained them until it / they were battered into submission. But it was and always has been the original and well-worn piece if fur on the long string that raises their hunting instinct like no other.

Uli and Nando must have been gladiators in a former life, because they fight each other twice a day. They always do this on the rug in the lounge and they never make a sound, even though their routine looks agonising. They will start off in a friendly enough way, with affectionate licking and the laying of paws on foreheads. Then, as if they are sounding each other out they circle and the occasional left arm jab will be thrown. Neither of them are southpaws. As the pace picks up, traditional boxing will turn into kick-boxing, followed by wrestling, with each grabbing the other in various head and arm locks as they roll around the rug. But drawing claws and ear and neck biting will be what decides who will be the loser. The pace will have been intense and so much fur will have been deposited on our designer rug that Mr. Dyson the vacuum cleaner will soon be made to clear up.

Fernando

Francesco, our champagne cat was the tallest cat we had, and the strongest. He was all muscle. Ants was muscular, but Franco was athletic as well. Uli, at over seven kilos is heavier, but because his legs are shorter he didn't appear to be as big and I'm sorry to say his weight is mostly fat, because apart from fighting with Nando, he does little exercise. Franco would eat the most out of all of them. He was what I term a "greedy-gobbly" and I used to think we were keeping a pig rather than a cat. God help us if we began to eat before he had been fed, because he would try to jump on the dining room table to pinch what we had on our plates.

Roger was fifteen when Franco, Uli and Nando appeared on the scene. Early on in his life Franco worked it out for himself that Roger was spoilt, because we gave Roger extra tit-bits the rest of our clowder weren't always getting. He was sharp enough to realise that if he hung out with Roger some of those tit-bits could end up in his bowl. Although Franco was a full brother to the two gingers, he was different in both looks and temperament. And where Uli's and Nando's coats are thick, soft and oily, his was short, coarse and dry. I kept telling him that if he didn't stop jumping on the table when we were eating, he would end up as a fireside rug.

Franco, we discovered couldn't meow. Instead, he quacked like a duck. He also made a long, high-pitched trumpet note. I would converse with him by blowing the same note out of the side of my mouth and he loved it. I tried to copy it precisely and he seemed to understand what I was saying, but I wish I understood what he was saying when he did it. Franco was his own man and it took him a couple of years to accept being stroked, because he interpreted the action as playing and when he played he liked to play rough. Playing rough with him was fun, but only up to a point. It would include him lying on his back, encouraging one of us to stroke his belly. To start with, he seemed to enjoy it, then, suddenly, he would grab hold of my intruding hand with his claws. Trying to pull it away was nigh impossible without having it severely scratched. Cats use the same action when toying with a rodent.

They hold it with their front paws and then gouge it to death with their back claws. Cats that are cared for will chase rodents for sport rather than for food and will torment them to death. Franco didn't differentiate between a hand and an unlucky rodent. All he wanted to do was to kill it. A cat's claws are angled inwards like shark's teeth and once a victim has been grabbed there is no escape. The best way we found to escape from his clutches was to pretend the hand is dead. When he felt no resistance he soon got bored. Another way to get away from Franco was to ask him to show mercy. Generally, he did.

Franco liked the computer mouse as well as real ones, or to be exact, the effects of the cursor on the screen created by the mouse. When the cursor was visible on the blank computer screen, he would try to grab it for as long as I was prepared to manipulate the mouse. He enjoyed boxing too. He would sit on his back legs like a kangaroo and we would spar with me, using my index fingers against his front paws. No gloves were worn. Paws have claws and fingers have nails, but claws always win.

He liked fish, and lots of it. He also liked meat, but if given the choice he would go for the fish every time. From experience he was well aware that if an onion was being peeled in the kitchen it was likely there would be other ingredients being prepared that were more to his liking. The rattle of pans and plates would also bring him to the kitchen when he was not wanted. More often than not, Franco's anticipation would be tinged with disappointment, because we are ninety per cent vegetarian and he didn't like veg.

He would groom my hair and scalp. The procedure took place as we were preparing to have an afternoon sleep. He would sit on the wide, padded arm of the divan where I rested my head after lunch and he would lick my hair for at least fifteen minutes, a few strands at a time, untangling them to his satisfaction.

He worked hard, never stopping for a break. It was dry licking, with no saliva. When he was satisfied my hair was clean and in place, he would work his way through to my scalp. Why he did it remains unclear. Maybe it was affection, or it could have been for the salt in my sweat. Whatever, he would have made a wonderful hairdresser.

When Roger died, the alpha cat mantle came up for grabs. Crewe Alexandra thought it was hers by right, but she only reigned for a short while, because Franco had other ideas. In his mind he was King. He took over and that was how it remained until he died. His demise came very suddenly and unexpectedly, and it was hard to believe, because he had been so powerful, fit and fast. He was five years old when one day I noticed he was starting to become fatter around his stomach. We thought it was middle-age spread, but within a month he was getting ridiculously fat and he was sleeping for too long. We took him to see Sandro, who told us that the prognosis was not good. He pushed a syringe into Franco's stomach to draw off some bile, which he sent to the laboratory. The results showed that his liver and both his kidneys were failing. Sandro said we had to keep an eye on him and if he stopped passing urine he would have to be put down, because he would be in pain. We took him back home to give him lots of special attention and cuddles but we knew, like he did, that our time together would be short.

Anybody who didn't know that he had gained weight wouldn't have known there was anything wrong with him. His weight gain didn't seem to slow him down much, but after a couple more weeks he stopped eating and drinking. One day, we were in the kitchen trying to tempt him to eat some tinned fish, which he would normally devour in seconds but he just sniffed at it and looked at us as if to say it was time for him to go. Nicola was literally moments away from telephoning Sandro to come and put him down when he walked out of the back door, past his brothers, Nando and Uli, who were sitting in the garden and started to climb the mountain at the back of the house. Nicola and I asked each other where he was going, but really we knew we wouldn't see him again. We'd never before had a cat that preferred to die his way. Of course we couldn't be certain he wouldn't come back. I scouted the less steep areas of the garden and the surrounding area in search of him, but after several hours of looking and a further twenty-four hours hoping for his return that never happened, we knew it was the end.

Franco

Sadness fell upon us once more. The pain of grief is the worst because there is nowhere to hide from it. It was such a sad scene watching him walk away, but I never gave up hope. I prayed for a miracle, that in a day or so he would come wandering down the mountain in his usual vigorous, energetic way and we could all be reunited in good health once again. But it wasn't to be. In some ways the ones that he had left behind helped cushion the blow, because they didn't seem to suffer his loss the way I do. Uli and Nando must have realised that their brother was missing but they didn't appear to grieve. All they did was sniff the spot where he used to sleep, looked at one another and effectively shrugged their shoulders. In some way this helped pick me up because they were philosophical about death. I guess that's how I must become.

Crewe hadn't see eye to eye with Franco and she was possibly the only one in our family who was glad to see the back of him. And after she had made many reconnaissance missions upstairs to check that he hadn't taken a vacation, she gradually began to move back into our apartment. After the latest bereavement we were now down to Crewe and three others, Stevie G, Uli and Nando and when Crewe was convinced Franco wasn't going to return she appointed herself as the alpha. She still regards my studio as her private domain but it has become what we term her "summer residence", because on very hot sunny days the studio remains cool. But whether she is in residence or not, she will guard the place for all she's worth against any of the others who get ideas about encroaching on her territory.

When Crewe was browbeating Kalash, my love for her waned, but in latter years we have become close, similar to the bond I had with Roger. It is understandable how she became the alpha and that is because she is remarkably sensible. She makes the others seem immature, even though she is only a year older. She's unfussy. I call her Madame, or Signora or sometimes an old granny. She's consistent, whereas the others are whimsical and look to me to mollycoddle them through life. That doesn't mean they aren't precious to me, because they are and I am to blame for bringing them up to be soft centred. Nevertheless, Crewe is all seeing, all-knowing; the others are her ignorant minions.

When Crewe moved back into our apartment it was lovely to be reunited. Naturally Uli, Nando and Stevie G had to readjust to accommodate her but everybody, including Nicola and me soon settled into a regular living pattern.

But if Crewe feels that at some point in her life she wants another change of location, the only place left for her is our guest apartment–but she'll need a key to get in.

12 Luis - The Squatter in the Loft

One winter's day in 2011, we saw a large and rather plump dark tabby sitting on the windowsill outside the kitchen. He had his black nose pressed against the glass and he was staring at us with his flashing green eyes. The sight of him gave us both a jolt. Because we hadn't seen another cat we didn't know so close to the house since the FIV carrier seven years earlier, so we were unsure about what to do. Nevertheless, we filled a bowl with tuna biscuits and with it, went to say hello. He didn't run away, but instead got stuck into the food. My first reaction was to shoo him away, because he might have been another FIV risk, or at least harbour some other disease or parasite. But I didn't, because he seemed to be friendly. When two of our cats saw him, rather than being intimidated by him, or acting in the anti-social way they usually do when a stranger approaches the house, they displayed no reaction. From that we concluded that they must know him.

He turned up again the next day and because it was winter and he was desperate for food, we gave him a bowl of meat. We couldn't tempt him into the house, but he did let us get close enough to see that he had scars from recent fights, canker in his ears and some fattened ticks on the back of his neck. From this, we surmised he had been roughing it for some time. We momentarily considered adopting him, but he left as soon as he had finished eating. Where he had come from we didn't know, and we don't know to this day. We described the mystery cat to some of our neighbours, but they didn't know anymore about him than we did.

For the rest of the winter we left a bowl of something on the patio for him, but if we forgot, he would sit on the windowsill, looking despondently at us. He wasn't aggressive in any way. He seemed to be a sweetie and I was fairly sure that he'd been abandoned because he had been neutered and he was comfortable with people. From that we guessed that he once belonged to someone who had died and he had been forced to leave his original home. I think that this happened some years ago and until he took up refuge with us he had been constantly on the move and the fact that he was not underfed when we first met him told us he had found at least a couple of homes where he could get food. Gradually, we were able to encourage him to come into the house to eat with the others, but our other cats weren't in favour of having a newcomer. For them, being outwardly friendly to him was fine if he was on the other side of the doorstep, but that extra metre into the kitchen was a step too far for our incumbents to accept. If he wanted to become a part of our family in any way, he would have to make his own arrangements.

Our villa has three floors with a self-contained apartment on each floor. The loft was designed so that a fourth apartment could be built into it and because we rent out some of our villa as holiday accommodation, we had plans drawn by an architect to convert it into an apartment. However, as the costs proved to be too much, we decided against it and we now use the space to store some sun-loungers and garden watering equipment. Consequently I don't go up there very often, but one day when I did, I discovered our visiting tabby asleep on one of the loungers. He had found a home for himself. The chimneystack from the pellet-burning stove in our apartment runs through the loft, so to make him more comfortable I put a large, fluffy cushion next to the chimneystack so that, should he stay for another winter he could get some warmth. He was still there a year later, a permanent squatter, which is not surprising, considering we had been feeding him twice a day. It was around this time we decided, albeit belatedly to give him a name.

Because he may already have a name given to him by his previous owners, we did doubt whether he would respond to it, but we thought it necessary to call him something. I got my suggestion in first and because his swarthy colouring I came up with Luis, after the fantastic Uruguayan striker Luis Suarez, whom Liverpool FC had recently bought. Amazingly there weren't any complaints from Nicola, apart from some silent head shaking and a disgusted look. So Luis it has remained.

Luis will allow us to stroke him lightly before he eats, but only before. To me, this proves that he must have been someone's domestic cat at some point in his life. Trying to pick him up is a different matter; he certainly won't allow that. Being raised of the ground can be a nasty shock for cats, especially the heavier ones. If their rib cage is squashed, breathing becomes difficult for them. Also, it's not hard to imagine how they must view someone who is fifteen times larger than they are who has this perverse need to keep lifting them off their feet. Even if it was done with kindness, we would be terrified if it happened to us and we would probably protest loudly. A cat that doesn't want to be held will wriggle like an eel, seemingly spinning around inside their own skin to escape with supreme ease. Given time, the majority of cats will get used to being picked up. Ants, Pam and Lele were our exceptions. They liked to be stroked but they refused to be picked up. Our ginger duo can be persuaded, but Nando isn't keen, so we don't try. Uli took his time to accept it, but with some gentle persuasion he eventually did and he became one of the soppiest we've had. But as he has become so heavy we cannot hold him for long. Franco also took his time, but he would be unpredictable and occasionally attack a hand. Roger was easy going and appreciated being carried about. Because of Stevie G's brutal start in life, I thought he would be the most unlikely cat to accept being picked up, but he enjoys it and asks me at least once a day to carry

him and when I do, I have to think of a new route around
the apartment to keep his interest. He likes me to open
cupboard and wardrobe doors at the higher level so he can
peer inside them. If we see Nicola on our journey, I will
announce that we are having a tour of the estate. Several
times I've thought of buying a harness for a human baby
so I can carry him around for longer periods, because after
ten minutes my arms will start to ache.

But I'm digressing. Because Luis wouldn't let us pick
him up, there was no way we were going to get him into a
cat carrier. That meant that we couldn't take him to Sandro
to get him checked over, so Sandro came over one day to
look at him. Even that was not easy. Luis really objected to
this close attention, but eventually Sandro managed to get
some drops onto Luis' neck and into his ears to help get
rid of the canker and the ticks.

Because our cats appear to know him, no doubt from
sorties in the woods and mountain they are not outwardly
aggressive towards him until he tries to enter the holy-of-
holies, our apartment. Then that is a different kettle of
fish. It's as if they cannot believe his impudence at
attempting to gate-crash their home. Nando sees our
allowing Luis into the apartment as a weakness, so when
Luis is close by, Nando will set up a border checkpoint.
Whenever he sees Luis, it's as if it's for the first time. His
bottom jaw will drop open, his eyes will widen in disbelief
and his tail will touch the floor. A drooping tail is an
unhappy tail, but Luis is thick-skinned and he knows that
at heart Nando is as soft as he is. All that takes place is a
lot of feline sabre-rattling, then after the ritual is over Luis
will creep past Nando, fill his face to his satisfaction as he
had intended and return to his fluffy cushion in the loft.

Cats not only protect what they regard as their terrain,
they also consider that they are protecting us. We have
become their property and to show this, they will mark our
clothes by rubbing the scent glands at the base of their tails
and at the sides of their necks against them. They will also

have marked the doorframes, table and chair legs, cushions, shoes, plant pots and most other objects that are at ground level, both inside and outside the house to warn a potential intruder not to come too close.

Surprisingly, Crewe seems to like Luis. As the alpha cat, she has never been warm-hearted towards what we term our "official" cats and she will order them about. Although she drove poor little Kalash out, she accepts Luis even when he hangs around my studio, which she guards heavily. Possibly it's because he is passive and he isn't interested in usurping her, or perhaps she fancies his swarthy Latin looks - who knows?

Luis

13 A Cat is for Life

From the time we first became cat carers, we have lived with twenty of them on a daily basis and cared for at least another twenty. At the time of writing (2017), two of our cats, Crewe Alexandra and Stevie G are coming up to twelve years old. The two marmalades, Uli and Nando are ten and a half. We can only guess the age of Luis, our squatter in the roof because he arrived without any documentation, but I'd say he was now around twelve. We've always wanted to have lots of animals and our wish has been well and truly granted. Sometimes I think it would have been nice to have had the opportunity to be selective about the ones we acquired, instead of them arriving via unfortunate circumstances but all the same we really enjoy having them around. If the expression, "it's a dog's life" describes a tough existence, we could coin the phrase "it's a cat's life", meaning the complete opposite. It's certainly the case with our cats. They have love and care in abundance, quality food, a knowledgeable and caring vet, for whose services they don't have to pay a cent, plus a choice of places to sleep in a villa that is set in one of the most beautiful and sought-after areas of Italy. I sometimes tell them they don't know how well off they are and perhaps a week or two living in an impoverished situation to remind them of how their lives used to be, or could have been, might make them more grateful.

Sometimes I think we have done the wrong thing by adopting more than one cat. Signora Luisa knows we are suckers for kittens and she will call us when she has some that need homes. We feel awful at having to turn her down, because a cat's life is at stake, but we have to be resilient and tell her we can't help her, that the cats we already have are set in their ways, they guard their territory tenaciously and they wouldn't like it if we introduced more cats into it. Being in a multi-cat household isn't what an individual cat wants and perhaps it comes down to selfishness on our part for wanting more than one. Nonetheless, we endeavour to keep our household harmonious. We've found that, despite the squabbles that arise over who gets the biggest share of my attention, as our cats age, they become more resigned to accepting others, especially when they realise they are not going short; that food and warmth are always in plentiful supply and perhaps it dawns on them that being possessive is a waste of effort.

Nicola has nicknamed me "The Pied Piper of Argegno," because our clowder will follow me wherever I go. When I tell people I have cats, they will ask me how many I have. I tell them I have five—four official and one unofficial (the unofficial one of course being Luis). They usually give me a quizzical look, but rather than ask what I mean by "official" and "unofficial", they will ask me why I keep so many. I think they ask because they want to see if I am some sort of eccentric, but whatever their reason, I always tell them that my reason for keeping so many is, when I have a yearning for the company of a cat, there is more of a chance that one of them will be around than if I just had one. I tell them my cats are my passion and I have dedicated my life to their happiness. This only mystifies them even more. Sometimes, they will ask me what use they are and I reply by asking them how many children they have. When they tell me, I'll ask them why they have them, and of what use they are. I'll then ask them if they have any passions and generally, they have: A man's passion might be watching or playing sport, like squash or golf. Or he might be into fast cars or model trains. A woman's might be shopping, baking, holidays abroad or eating out. They like those things and I love our cats. So who is the most extreme, or even odd in their passions? In my opinion, caring for cats is a far more rewarding exercise than following trivia.

I've found that people who aren't cat lovers are suspicious of men like me. It's acceptable for some madcap old woman to have a houseful of cats, but not for a man. It's fortunate for me that I have a wife who, if called upon will vouch that I am not some sort of deviant. Also, my being an artist doesn't get me many bonus points in respect of being a cat lover, because a lot of people consider artists to be oddballs too. Some people cast aspersions on the masculinity or even the sexuality of a man who has an association with cats, but they have no doubts if a man has a lot of dogs. They might say it enhances his masculinity. 'A proper man's animal, the dog,' they'll say. 'But a man with five cats, now that's weird!'

I find it hard to communicate with people who find animals odious and I'm sure that if I ever caught anybody harming an animal, I would try to harm the assailant. The officers of animal protection organisations like the RSPCA should be given the power of arrest, rather than only gather evidence and prosecute offenders privately. I've seen commercials on TV asking for donations to assist in animal welfare. There are societies requiring money to halt the trafficking of rare species. There are other organisations that save maltreated dogs, donkeys, horses and cats, all of which have to rely on public support to survive. I believe it is scandalous that governments are not being forced to do the funding.

Nicola and I are not just surrogate parents; our life is dedicated to our cats' happiness and contentment. As an example of that dedication, in 2011 we allowed ourselves a holiday, which was the first one we'd had since we'd arrived in Italy twenty years earlier. It wasn't through misfortune or lack of funds that we'd not taken one, but because we don't like having to be away from our cats for too long, in case they fret. We only took the chance to see other parts of our adopted country because we found trustworthy cat-sitters. An English couple, Claire and

Martin had rented our first floor holiday apartment.

We got to know them so well that we had the idea of offering them a cat minding deal. If they were prepared to stay in our house to look after our cats when we took a holiday, we would give them free holiday accommodation in the apartment. They readily agreed and the following year, they took up our offer and we were able to take our holiday.

We drove to the Marche region for three days, continued down the east side of Italy to Puglia and then cut across to Basilicata. We then drove to the foot of Italy, to Calabria, where we had a wonderful time. We telephoned Claire and Martin several times to see how they were coping with baby-sitting, partly because I was worried that our cats would miss us, but they said they seemed to be fine. Claire and Martin returned two years later to cat-sit when we visited Sicily.

It's been my experience that cats born in the wild never really take to strangers. If a stranger comes to our house, our cats will run outside immediately, almost tripping the individual up in their haste to get away, or they will hide under the bed until the coast is clear. Roger was one that was more tolerant of strangers and because he was so pretty, most of them wanted to touch him. Reluctantly he would let them, but anyone could tell he didn't like it.

I'm convinced that cats are telepathic. If we have to make an appointment for any of them to see the vet, they make sure they are hard to find. All too often I have had to phone Sandro to cancel an appointment because the cat in question already knew about the appointment and has disappeared. Although I joke about this, I'm sure there is an extra sense they have and I wonder if that may be why cats have long been associated with witches and with the occult. As a teenager I used to go mountain trekking in North Wales and on one of those trips I came across a travelling fair, which had been set up in a valley. There, a gypsy fortune-teller was selling her skills. She had a black cat sitting on the edge of her table and after she had read my palm we started to talk about cats. The gypsy said she was a psychic and used the power of her cat to communicate with spirits.

Certainly the ancient Egyptians believed that cats had psychic powers and venerated them for it. It is commonly believed they were the first race to domesticate cats. Cats were a sacred part of Egyptian religion and they believed a cat bestowed the same life giving qualities as the sun. They also believed the glow of a cat's eyes reflected solar rays, thereby elevating it to the status of a God. They made laws against anyone killing a cat, even accidentally and if anyone were caught doing so they would incur the death penalty and instantly. When a cat died their bodies were mummified with great care and ceremony.

When I lived by myself in Surrey, I did a job for a client who lived not far from me. She told me she was a divorcee and had got rid of her husband because her cats were allergic to him. She told me she wasted too much time tending to, and sleeping with her cats. She had three when at the time I didn't have any, but I remember thinking even then, why should she think it a waste of time when it is one of life's better pleasures? Our cats agree with me on this. The moment when I sit down to relax is what they have waited for all day. They will swamp me and demand attention in the form of kisses and cuddles and they will all want it at the same time. I try to distribute my attention equally, but I only have one pair of hands and if I leave any of them out, they will get jealous and complain. Sometimes, if Nicola is nearby I will ask her to lend a hand and she will try her best to satisfy their needs, but it's really me they want and they will look over at me and know they have been off-loaded. I've said before that cat's have an unlimited amount of patience when it comes to stalking prey, but, as with food, when it comes to stroking and cuddling they want it there and then.

Although I have said that our cats seem to have

become more relaxed about sharing space with each other as they get older, their jealousy, or perhaps it's their possessiveness, in respect of getting my attention seems to have intensified with age. I thought that with them having long-term security it would diminish, but they actually compete with one another more. They will watch intently to see how much of it is being dispensed and to whom and if I am not giving them attention in equal measure, their eyes will become enlarged and they will fight like a boxer, each giving the cat that they think is getting more than their fair share, a bashing. Muhammad Ali based his technique on watching how cats box and in finding inspiration from them he became 'The Greatest.' If a cat's punch is well timed it can make the cat at which it is aimed, reel. I was once on the end of a cat punch that missed its intended target. It bruised my forearm. It's a boxer's hook for sure.

During our daily post lunchtime *riposo* (the Italian equivalent of the Spanish siesta) on the divan, it's important for me to make sure I am comfortable before they climb on top of me. If I start to wriggle around to find a better position they will complain and sometimes one of them will give me an impatient bash with a paw. But swamped as I may be, and as comfortable and warm as we are the time always comes when I have to get up and get on with my work. It's a shame to have to push my cats to one side, but it has to be done. They don't understand, or maybe they don't want to understand. They will try their best to keep me where I am by making themselves as heavy as they can. After all, I am their electric blanket and they are not best pleased if the warmth is about to be switched off. To them, nothing in the world can possibly be more urgent than having a kiss, a cuddle and sometimes a massage until we are exhausted from the effort of it all. They are right. There is nothing better. Shunning love and affection is regrettable. Our time together is short. I am aware of how special they are and when I'm with them I realise how transient life is. But getting on with work depends on how pressing time may be. If it is something that can wait, it has been known for them to win. Am I wasting time? I don't think so.

Where I am lax with our cats, Nicola is firm. They know that when Nicola is being firm, and is firm in a way they understand, they know they have to behave, or else! I don't see the point of being firm. Our cats are our babies and I am their daddy. We look forward to having a nice time together, which to me doesn't mean being firm.

Apart from plucking at our very expensive divan, in my eyes my cats don't do anything reprehensible. I allow them, within the bounds of hygiene to do what they want, where they want, when they want. This annoys Nicola and she tells me not to give them what they want all the time, otherwise they will ride roughshod over me. The consequence of Nicola being firm is they don't love her as much as they love me. She blames me for being besotted with cats. She tells me I am weak and that they need some discipline, but I say, weak about what? And does it matter? I ask her if she remembers how weak she was when she was in love. She tells me not to be so stupid.

She's right when she says they run roughshod over me, but I don't care. I agree I am besotted and I am weak, but I cannot help it and our cats know I am a soft touch. They know how to twist me around their little paws and they know I will let them. Cats know how to weave spells and they entranced me years ago. Covetousness, self-indulgence and maliciousness are characteristics of which we humans are instructed early on in life to rid ourselves. Religious teachings such as we may read in the Bible mark these out as socially unacceptable, but cats behave how we would behave if such instruction hadn't been pumped into us. I said earlier that Nicola's parents kept dogs. Sometimes, if she sees one of our cats doing what she regards is misbehaving she will set out to try and teach them some "decorum" by using tried and trusted dog training methods. These are alien to a cat and they will look at her as if she's gone nuts. She has then to accept that she's not winning.

We brush our cats and they usually adore it as much as they enjoy being stroked and cuddled. We brush them more in the summer, because they catch burrs in their coats and if they have been rolling in dry earth to keep parasites at bay, they spread the dust and the burrs around the house. They can be hesitant about being brushed if they suspect we are going to do it only to remove burrs or searching for ticks; they know instantly the difference between being brushed for pleasure and being examined, and they don't like being examined. We can alleviate their suspicion if we tickle them under their chins as we examine them, but if they feel they haven't been pleasured to their own satisfaction, they'll wander off in a huff, feeling mightily disappointed.

I can spend hours watching our cats when they are asleep. It is both a wonderful and a comical sight. As a prelude to sleep, they will indulge themselves in a thorough washing and licking session. Then, if it is winter they will cuddle together on our bed, creating balls of breathing fur. Bottoms will be close to faces; whiskers will touch ears and make them twitch; tails and paws will entwine in so much of a jumble that it can take a while to work out to whom they belong. Nicola says, 'don't they just melt your heart?' I tell her we are fortunate to be blessed with such a beautiful family. And if that sounds like a piece of sentimental corn, it's meant to.

Cats can be unashamedly decadent when it comes to comfort and they don't care what time of day or night they indulge themselves, or how long they spend doing so. Cats love to lie on wool, especially in the winter months and the thicker the wool, the sounder they sleep. We give ours old sweaters or blankets to sleep on. If I see our cats piled on top of each other asleep I will start to feel drowsy and before long I'm lying down next to them. If I'm wearing a thick woollen sweater they will wake up and pile on top of me to carry on with their sleep.

I have never known a cat suffer insomnia. They sleep during the day, whilst most of us work and I reckon they have it the right way round. Even though I have spent the best years of my life in the company of cats, I still haven't decided if they go to bed late and get up late or go to bed early and get up early, because if clocks control mankind, they certainly don't control cats.

Our cats will sleep soundly until breakfast time at five o'clock. Then they insist that Nicola or I present them with what they fancy. Generally, Nicola volunteers me to do the presenting. Crewe, the alpha cat will want serving first and she will order a small bowl of milk, followed by trout and rice flavoured biscuits. The others will be waiting as patiently as they can for me to serve them. While they are waiting I will open the back door to let in Luis, our upstairs cat and together they will consume a sachet of meat each, followed by either the standard trout and rice biscuits or perhaps beef flavoured ones or, occasionally, salmon. They will then wash it all down with fresh water. When they've eaten their lot they will drift outside to follow scent trails. If the trails are fresh they may return with presents for us.

None of them are backward in coming forward when it comes to letting me know if the service I provide isn't up to standard. Years ago I learnt the lesson never to try introducing cheaper foods into their diet. When I have, they have kicked up a great hullabaloo. Once a cat has been introduced to better food brands there is no way it will downgrade. Our adopted ferals, which at one time in their lives would have eaten anything thrown in their direction and be grateful for it are now food snobs. Nicola says I'm a fool for allowing them to take over. I say what the hell. Living in the same environment as another creature is an experience to be savoured.

We of course give our cats a balanced diet. Every week

I buy lots of different brands and flavours of *crocchette* (cat biscuits), otherwise they get bored, but their favourite is the Ultima brand of *trota e riso* (trout and rice) and if I don't provide it when they expect it they will stage a sit-down protest. The supermarket where I buy the biscuits quite frequently runs out of stock of this flavour, which is highly inconvenient because it means I have to scout other supermarkets well outside my normal shopping route to find them. God forbid if I come back empty handed.

They don't all go for tinned cat meat. Some cats can be gluttons for it, whereas others are content with cat food sachets or biscuits. On the other hand, Crewe is reluctant to eat anything but trout and rice biscuits, bits of chopped up cheese and sachets of meat. And of course, for her, the meat has to be from a freshly opened sachet. Over the years, proprietary cat food has improved greatly and nowadays the pet food section in supermarkets is packed with different varieties. I suppose the flavour has too; I haven't actually tasted any myself to find out, but without doubt our clowder is definitely more enthusiastic about food than they used to be. They used to prefer tinned food and some found biscuits uninteresting, but now, for most of them the reverse seems to be true. The market for pet foods is nowadays is so vast it is worth billions per year. Back in the very brief time I had Whiskers, there were, I think only one brand of cat biscuit and one brand of tinned food available. Most people made their own pet food, buying cheap cuts of meat and offal from the butcher then boiling it for hours or feeding them on scraps and leftover human food. Perhaps cat food manufacturers have been responsible for the rise in the number of domestic cats in the world, which is estimated to be around 600,000,000. Now that cat food is readily available and easy to serve, feeding a cat is undoubtedly less effort than it used to be.

It amuses me to see a bowl of left over spaghetti outside a front door for the feral cats of Argegno. Even though human food is not supposed to be good for cats, the residents who put it out probably don't know that and they believe that giving the ferals something to eat is better than not giving them anything. If I presented our cats with spaghetti, they would stage a sit-down protest, (apart from Stevie G of course who seems to relish it), accompanied by a disgusted look that tells me they expect better.

There once was an advert for a well-known brand of cat food that showed a close up of a cat about to eat from a bowl, with a caption saying, "a cat's stomach is only the size of a man's thumb." What they don't say is that a cat's stomach can stretch to the size of a man's fist when it's full of food. Our weekly shopping list seems to show more items of cat food on it than food for us two. And when I place the cat food on the checkout counter I can get some peculiar looks from both the checkout girl and shoppers waiting in the queue behind me. Times have been hard in Italy lately and a lot of pensioners are being forced to buy the minimum at discount prices in order to survive. Perhaps they think we are so hard up that we've had to resort to eating cat food.

I didn't realise until I had cats that smell travels at the speed of light. A cat, or in our case cats might not be in sight of the tin of cat food, but if one of us should open a tin of something they like, they will be rubbing round our legs before the lid is off. They will then sit in the most inconvenient places on the kitchen floor, just in case we are likely to forget what it is we are doing, causing us to stumble and re-focus our intentions on feeding them.

Nicola upset the apple cart one day, but I paid the price for it, because initially it was my fault. When I went to do the big weekly food shop I forgot to buy cat food sachets. This was a serious mistake on my part. I called Nicola while she was on the train home, to ask her to buy some in Como town centre before she got on the ferryboat to Argegno. She was well aware of the alarm, because without sachets in stock we wouldn't get any peace. The trouble began when she opened her rucksack to reveal twelve tins of Sheba. Our cats may be cute, cuddly "daddy's darlings", but they are also gutbuckets. I intentionally avoid buying Sheba because from past experience I know that all cats go crazy for it. Once a tin of Sheba has been opened, they don't know when to stop eating it and once they have tasted Sheba they won't accept any other brands. Nicola says they must put something in it to "hook" cats.

If we have Sheba in the house they become unsettled and when they say 'please sir can we have some more' if I think they have had sufficient, I will ignore their pleas and they will hate me for it. The other day, four of them were sitting in line across the kitchen floor and I swear they were chanting 'we want Sheba! We want Sheba!' It took a lot of time and patience on my part to get them to downgrade to their usual brand once the Sheba was finished.

Springtime can be wet in the north of Italy. Uli and Nando excepted, our cats don't like *il maltempo* - the bad weather. They dislike wet grass touching their bellies, so we have stepping-stones across the garden to help them avoid it. Springtime is moulting time, which means Mr. Dyson the vacuum cleaner will have his work cut out. Vacuuming the apartment is a non-stop job and the cats hate Mr. Dyson. We also have Roomba the robot vacuum cleaner and they hate him even more. When Roomba is doing his rounds they will stare at him as if he's an intruder. He's about the same size as they are, but because his programme is unpredictable they cannot fathom out where he's going or what he's doing. In fact, he has us all fooled. He can return to his dock and re-charge himself, then burst into action unannounced, which has our cats running for the nearest open door or window to escape his tiresome interference. Only when they are sure he is in sleep mode will they creep back.

Cats are sun worshippers and their character changes when the summer temperatures arrive. They will become happy cats and they spend hours sunbathing. I believe Italian cats are twice as happy as British cats because they get twice the amount of sun. Italian people are the same. I like the warmth of the summer, but it will mean our cats will be outside. On summer nights they will sleep either on the terrace under the veranda, or further up the mountain, on the flattened patches of high grass they use for daytime sleeps rather than on our bed, their favourite spot in winter. Also in the summer they are less likely to share an afternoon riposo on the divan.

Our winters are not severe, despite night time temperatures falling to as low as four degrees above zero. I like wintertime best, certainly not for the weather but because our cats are at their cuddliest. All our cats, apart from the hyperactive marmalades more or less hibernate during the winter. They will hog the central heating radiators or the top of the pellet-burning stove for as long as it is fired up, waking only for food or to go outside to relieve themselves. It always amazes me how they can go from the sweltering heat of the stove to the cold outside and not suffer the consequences later on. If the weather is indifferent, they prefer to lay their heads on our bed. Trying to do housework in the mornings can be difficult; I don't want to disturb them, particularly when it comes to bed making and vacuum cleaning, so the jobs will be postponed until an hour or two around lunch time when the room has been vacated. In the evening they snuggle into us while we watch the television, before we all transfer ourselves to our bed to carry on snuggling. Our poor overloaded bed has to wait until the summer heat arrives to get a break. Nicola says that hotel beds have it easy compared to ours.

On a winter's night our bedroom is a sight to behold. Nicola goes to bed a lot earlier than I do because she has to be up early to get to her office in Milan. If don't get to bed by ten o'clock, which I rarely do, I will struggle to find a space to sleep, because the bed will be covered in cats.

There will be little or no space for me to squeeze in, but when I do, within a couple of minutes Uli will snuggle into my neck and start licking my face, my ears and especially my fingers. He licks me so much I tell him there will be nothing left of me if he carries on. I let him do this for around five minutes, but then I have to turn over, because I'm no longer able to stand the heat from his body. Then he'll move onto my pillow so he can still be near me.

I once placed a thermometer between two sleeping cats to see how high the temperature rose. After four minutes, it read thirty-eight degrees. This business of our cats sleeping on our bed started when they were kittens. We took them to bed with us to keep them safe and warm, but nowadays they are there before we are and it's us that have to find a space to keep safe and warm. With a combined weight of twenty-plus kilos they pin us down and they don't like it if we try to move. Nicola says, 'who needs contraception if they have four cats sleeping on them?

Because our villa sits between the lake shore and the woodland that covers the mountains, we have enough animals living in or passing through our premises to enable us to open a wildlife park. All we'd have to do is coax them into pens and I'm sure the public would pay to see them. The birds that visit us would keep ornithologists entertained; sometimes they land in our garden or on the terrace while we are sitting out. Depending on the season, anyone visiting the woods behind our villa will see every species of bird common to central Europe, including woodpecker, jay, kingfisher, cuckoo and plenty of rare songbirds. Later in the year, black kites will swoop down from great heights to catch fish from the lake. Some of the mallard ducks that reside on the lake visit us regularly. Visitors will also see and hear the rooster from our neighbour Rico's hencoop, which will land in one of our six-metre high palm trees and sit in its dense leaves for a few hours, clucking contentedly. Our cats get very excited when a bird lands in the garden, so we can be kept pretty busy saving the lives of these little avians.

At night, three roe deer visit regularly as well as, but not at the same hour as two wild boar. In the afternoon two wild goats pay us a visit, as do all manner of reptiles, rodents and insects. The deer and the goats come in to lop the tops off my flowers and lettuces and just about everything else they find edible, whilst the boar come to dig up my root vegetables. No matter how big these invaders are, our cats show no fear of them.

Our bedroom window is in a sheltered spot under the awnings of the villa and if the weather is mild, the cats will jump in and out of it of during the night. In the winter of 2016, a roe stag began sleeping under this window. We knew he was there because we could see his antlers above the window ledge. His size didn't bother our cats at all and they leapt over him as if he wasn't there.

The latest addition to our menagerie isn't a cat, but he steals the cats' food. He is Rico's very large and very friendly yellow Labrador, who bounds around our garden as if he owns it. He's so big and powerful it's impossible to argue with him, so we just have to wait until he decides to go back up the mountain to his home. He also steals our shoes, slippers and gardening gloves. Like all dogs, he has an acute sense of hearing, so when we are outside, especially when I'm cutting the grass with a strimmer he will make an appearance. I think he thinks I'm playing and he tries to join in.

According to the theory that within a year a single cat will eliminate all creatures smaller than itself within a hundred metre radius of where it lives, we ought to be free of mice, lizards, snakes, scorpions, slow worms, crickets, moles, voles and the rest, but in the area around us, this isn't the case. We have lived in this villa since 2004, yet our cats still regularly rock up with various examples of the above on a regular basis. Their favourite present is a disembowelled rat. In the summer they bring home grass snakes. They don't pull them to bits, but will whirl them around their heads, in which case I have to intervene to try and rescue these poor reptiles while they are still alive.

When one or all of our cats return from a hunting expedition, any trophy they bring back will be in one of three conditions. The first condition is dead but intact, the second is dead and disembowelled and the third is very much alive. Given the choice, I would prefer them dead and intact. Partially dissected is my second choice, but it means there will be a trail of blood and guts to clean up.

A live victim is the worst, because it can run and hide and make my life difficult. One rat was very much alive when one of our little darlings placed it on the kitchen floor for us to admire. The rat took this interlude in activity to take off at top speed and it ended up inside a wardrobe in our bedroom. After two days trying to persuade the very reluctant creature to come out, I had to dismantle the wardrobe to get at it. We had to wash or dry clean all the clothes that were in there to get rid of the mess it left behind.

Early one summer's morning I came face to face with the most unwelcome of visitors. I had got up to go to the bathroom and I hadn't switched on the light, because there was enough moonlight coming through a window at the end of the corridor for me to see where I was going. On my way back to bed, I saw what could have been a pair of shoes or an item of clothing on the floor, which I thought was odd, because neither Nicola nor I would leave anything there. I switched the light on to take a proper look at this object.

It was a snake. And it was a big one.

The corridor is less than a metre and a half wide, which meant that my bare feet must have been very close to it. It was tightly coiled against the skirting board, which might explain why I hadn't stepped on it. I took a closer look to see what type of snake it was and to see if it was injured or dead. It was an adder, the only venomous snake native to

Italy, and it was very much alive. What to do now?

Although the back door had been left open to let in some cool air, I was certain it hadn't got into the house of its own accord. One of our cats, or maybe two must have brought it in, but what was strange was there were no cats around. Normally when they have brought live prey into the house they torment it until they decide it is time to deliver the fatal bite. Maybe they had got fed up of this one because it had remained coiled up and hadn't been much fun.

To me, the snake looked very disgruntled, or maybe it always looked that way. Not being an expert on snakes, I wouldn't know. No matter; it was neither the time nor the place for a discourse on a snake's facial expressions. What I did know was that I was the one who would have to take it out of the house and this wasn't the normal run of the mill creature to dispose of. This was serious!

I am well practised in the techniques of the disposing of animals, alive or dead in the early hours, including grass snakes, but they are small in comparison to this one. This one was a proper snake and it was its size that gave me a jolt. Although grass snakes are quick movers, they can be trapped with little difficulty using a long handled dustpan and brush. Dealing with this one could be an altogether different experience and one that had to be given some thought before I attempted to get rid of it, otherwise I could end up in hospital with a serious snakebite.

I considered asking Nicola to give me a hand. She was asleep, no more than ten metres away, but to wake her up I would have had to walk past the snake again, or call out to her. This could have aroused the creature more than it was already roused and it was already beginning to uncoil itself. The situation demanded immediate action, because it might find a place to hide that could make disposing of it a lot more difficult than it was already. So, I fetched my trusty long handled dustpan and brush from the utility room and stood as far back as possible, in case it decided to strike.

As soon as it saw the brush approaching it coiled itself up again. This gave me the chance to get it onto the dustpan without a struggle, which was encouraging because once coiled it became lethargic, but it was so heavy it bent the handle and slid off. Fortunately, it let me have another go at picking it up. Now I was aware of its weight, which I estimated was around two kilo's, so rather than lift it up and carry it, I tipped the dustpan back and sort of pushed and slid it along the tiled floor, holding the snake in place with the brush.

Within a matter of seconds I managed to get it into the garden, but when we had gone only a metre from the back door it slid off the dustpan once more. This was not good. Any live creature needs to be taken as far away from the house as possible, hopefully without a cat in attendance, because if one of them were around it would call the others to assist in recapturing it and re-presenting it. So, once more I scooped it up and dumped it well away from the house, behind a rosemary bush. Then I shut the back door and the cat flap so neither it nor anything else could get in.

I returned to bed, but during the moments before I fell asleep I considered how I might not be lying there if the disposal process had gone wrong. I thought how cats never fail to make life challenging. I also wondered if Nicola would believe me when I told her that we'd had a very unwelcome visitor during the night. Maybe I should have taken a selfie as proof.

Nicola and I have often complimented one another on what a fine-looking family we have accumulated. We have always got on very well with our adopted children and continue to do so and they have always got on with us and continue to do so; unfortunately they don't always get on with one another as well as we would like them to and it sometimes seems that they tolerate one another out of convenience. I'm sure if they were asked individually whether they prefer to share, they would say no.

All the same I would sooner be with my cats than anywhere else. Besides being my best friends they are my playmates, and save for when we are asleep I am mindful enough to appreciate every second of our waking moments together. I have to admit they enthral me and I let them do anything they like.

If they were human, they would be considered as being spoilt to death and they would probably end up being obnoxious adults.

They want for nothing, because they deserve it.

14 My Last Will and Testament

My daughter, Sammie telephoned recently for a news update and during the conversation she enquired after our cats. After I told her, she told me she had just read an article in a newspaper about a deceased lady in Wales who had left all her money (one million pounds) in her will, to be divided evenly between her five cats. She said how strange the woman must be because how can cats spend money?

She went silent when I told her that Nicola and I intend doing something similar when we pop our clogs, except we are going to leave it all to a deserving cats home in exchange for an assurance that any cats we leave behind will receive consummate attention for the rest of their lives.

It was actually a tease and my daughter knew it was. She knows that by Italian probate law she is entitled to a third of my estate with a third going to my wife, leaving me with a third to do with as I wish. At this stage in our lives, my last third is likely to be going to a cats' home.

Discover Paul Wright's Other Books on Amazon

The first book of the Italian trilogy is
An Italian Home - Settling by Lake Como

"Paul Wright's tribute to the robust pleasures of village life brings out the generosity and humanity of the inhabitants of Lake Como" Desmond O'Grady, Italian Insider Review

Just what is it like for a foreigner to live and work in a northern Italian village, and become part of the community? How tough is it to leave your home country and settle in a new one? What do you have to do to be accepted by the people who live in a village that has existed for over five hundred years? Award-winning and stage designer and artist Paul Wright and his partner Nicola found out the hard way, working, playing, laughing, eating and drinking alongside the residents of a beautiful lakeside village.

Available in Kindle and in paperback

The sequel to An Italian Home is
An Italian Village - a Perspective on Life beside Lake Como

"An insightful and often funny depiction of Italian Life"
Hannah McIntyre, The Italian Insider Magazine

In this, the follow up to his successful book, 'An Italian Home', Paul relays more enthralling real-life stories about Italian village life. His regular dialogue with a group of people who have retired, mostly from the catering trade who occupy the granite seating around the village fountain on a daily basis, punctuates his adventures beyond the village boundaries for all manner of clients, both reputable and not so reputable in the surrounding area and beyond, to the Italian Riviera.

Available in Kindle and in paperback